Legal

Edition 1.2

Written by Bob D'Eith

Printed in the United States of America

First Printing, 2014

ISBN 10 149222975X
ISBN 13 9781492229759

Adagio Music Inc.
dba Adagio Media
100-938 Howe Street
Vancouver, B.C.
Canada V6Z 1N9
www.adagiomusic.ca
www.bobdeith.com

D1534507

TABLE OF CONTENTS

ACKNOWLEDGEMENTS

It would be impossible to thank the many people who have helped me to accumulate my knowledge of music and the music business, however I would be remiss if I did not acknowledge the people that sparked a life-long passion for music early on: Ellen Silverman, Bobby Doyle, Rob Karr, Peter Taylor, and the late Marjorie Maybe. I have to thank Paul Schmidt, my partner in Mythos, for renewing my love for making music at a time when I might have thrown in the towel.

On the business side of things, I have drawn on the wisdom of many people, but I have to single out my friend and former business partner Marc LaFrance who introduced me to Music BC and eventually helped me land the position as executive director (and thanks for taking me to Abbey Road Studios in London, that was truly awe inspiring). At Music BC, I have had the privilege of working with some incredible board members who are too numerous to name. I should, however, mention one name. Early on at Music BC, I was mentored by one of our executives, Gary Russell, from Standard Broadcasting. He taught me a lot about running an organization, helped me to understand how radio broadcasting and CRTC regulations work and generally saved our collective skin on numerous occasions from a funding point of view.

Other than bringing the JUNO Awards to Vancouver, being asked to create the Peak Performance Project has been one of my proudest moments. Gerry Siemens and the Jim Pattison Broadcast Group allowed me to fulfill a vision for the BC indie music scene that still seems too amazing to be true. The program has taught hundreds of artists about the music business and funded dozens of bands. I have also learned a great deal from my experiences with the PPP and all of that knowledge is reflected in this book.

And for those people who stood in my way, criticized me, tried to bring me down, cheated me out of money or otherwise acted unethically – thank-you – I learned from you all that I know about the dark side of the music business. And unfortunately, there is a dark side. I have chosen never to be bitter, but to enjoy the wonderful parts of this crazy music world.

As far as the book itself, thanks to Gerilee McBride for the book artwork and design. Special thanks to Angelo Dodaro, Stuart Popp, Kurt Dahl, Savannah Wellman and Tarra Wandler for the feedback and proofing. Also, thanks to Maureen Jack from Music Books Plus for making me take my own advice that there is no such thing as good writing, only good re-writing.

Of course, I have to thank my children Sheldon, Braden, Cameron, Amy, Aryn and my amazing wife Kim for being so understanding especially in regard to my crazy travel schedule.

Our relationships help to shape our lives and I am deeply indebted to the people who have been part of my journey.

FORWARD BY GRANT LAWRENCE

"If you want to see the world, join a band".

That's one of my all-time favourite music biz quotes. I'm pretty sure Fat Mike said it, the lead singer of the ageless San Francisco pop-punk band NoFX. I like the quote because it's true. At least...it eventually came true in a very real sense for me. I formed my own band when I was a teenager. Through extremely hard work, constant trial and error, massive disappointment, persistence, and luck, we did manage to tour to many far off parts of the planet, just like Mike said. We did it all without the help of a major label, and in some cases, even a booking agent. But I have to admit...it would have been a hell of a lot smoother if I knew someone like Bob D'Eith way back then.

Bob D'Eith has dedicated his life to helping you, the musician. Many times, Bob and I have had discussions on how emerging artists can cut through the immense noise and competition, just to be seen and heard. From strictly a media perspective (the world I now come from at CBC), the #1 tip I can offer an emerging musician in our age of communication is: make yourself as accessible as possible. As a member of the music media hoping to discover you, I want all of your up-to-the-minute materials - bio, songs, video, tour dates - available to me at as few "clicks" as possible.

Bob D'Eith gets this. In fact, as you are about to read, Bob understands far, far more about the music business that I ever could. For the past quarter century, Bob has done it all. He's been a musician, a recording studio owner, a music publisher, the longtime executive director of Music BC, a chairman of FACTOR NAB, a JUNO rep, and is one of the co-founders of BC's hugely successful artist development Peak Performance Project. Most importantly, Bob is an entertainment lawyer. He knows exactly what you as an artist can and cannot do, legally speaking. It doesn't get any more clear-cut than that.

I'm very glad that my friend Bob finally decided to get off his lazy ass to write this book. It needed to be written. I just wish he had done it 25 years earlier. It would have made my life as an independent musician much, much easier. Tap into his knowledge, enjoy the ride, and maybe even buy him a beer. He deserves it.

Grant Lawrence
Host/Producer/Author
CBC Music Vancouver

A CAREER IN MUSIC:

The other 12 step program

(First Canadian Edition)

Part 1: The other 12 step program

INTRODUCTION

Sometimes I wonder if being bitten by the music bug is a blessing or a curse. If you are a professional musician, then you know what I mean. Once you have tasted the forbidden fruit of a life in music, it is difficult to ignore for very long. Most of my professional musician friends have struggled valiantly for years and some have prospered, but many have not. A very, very small number have skyrocketed to superstardom. The one thing they have in common is that they all started as independent artists.

As a lawyer, I can bill hundreds of dollars an hour. As a musician, I sell songs on iTunes for $0.99 a song. What is more satisfying? Honestly, the sale of one album for $10 is far more personally rewarding than billing an hour as a lawyer. When I am old and grey, I am not going to pine for the days when I used to draft contracts, my fondest memories will come from the days that I toured and created music in the studio.

It is the ability to create that separates human beings from other animals in the world. That is what we are put on earth to do. That is what our decedents will remember from our time. That is why music is so important.

Why listen to me? What qualifies me to give you advice? As a Canadian, I am naturally humble, so please indulge me while I establish my credibility. I have been a musician my entire life. I have had deals that associated me with major labels such as A&M/Universal, Warner and Virgin/EMI. I have toured extensively and recorded and released 8 records as an artist through the bands Rymes with Orange and Mythos. My record sales are in the 6 figures. I have won and been nominated for a number of awards including two WCMA wins and two JUNO Awards nominations. I have had top 10 radio hits and charted for many months in Billboard magazine in the USA. I have jammed with The Trews at the Canadian ambassador's house in Tokyo and have been asked to play on the stage at JUNO Awards after parties and other music industry events with guys from Hedley, Mother Mother, Wide Mouth Mason, Simple Plan, Odds, Chilliwack and many others. I have had a very colourful and interesting career in music and enjoyed every minute of it.

On the business side, I have been a music lawyer for over two decades, and spent significant time as the president of two record label/publishing companies. Additionally, I have represented hundreds of artists, various labels, publishers, managers and agents and have seen some of my clients attain incredible success in the business.

For over a decade, I have run the Music BC Industry Association, which is dedicated to nurturing and developing musicians and the music industry in my province. This has played an integral part in the development of my knowledge base and has introduced me to the world of funding and music business education. Music BC has been very fortunate to work with private radio to develop various programs, among them, the award winning Peak Performance Project; a $5.2 million artist development program run in BC.

I have also been on the FACTOR national advisory board for many years and this has given me unique insight into how FACTOR and other funding organizations work. FACTOR is the Foundation to Assist Canadian Talent on Recordings and is a major funder of musicians and music companies in Canada. I have also served on the boards of the Canadian Independent Music Association (CIMA) and the Council of Canadian Music Industry Associations (CCMIA). I serve as a director of the WCMA and BreakOut West award show, conference and music festival.

My goal was always to make 100% of my living from music. I am very proud of the fact that one-way or the other, this goal has been achieved. I have to wear a lot of hats, but that seems to be the nature of the beast.

This book is about survival in one of the most difficult professions that I know. It is aimed at professional musicians, bands and people who are seeking a meaningful career in music.

WHERE THE RUBBER HITS THE ROAD

We are all so busy. Our attention spans have gotten so short that we want instant gratification. Unfortunately, the music business is not a quick study. The learning curve to understand the business is very steep and with new trends it is changing daily. Acquiring a sufficient knowledge base can seem daunting, especially to a musician who has spent all of his or her time perfecting the craft of performance. Knowledge is power. I hope that I can impart some of that to you over the course of this book.

While I can't tell you how to succeed for sure - there is no magic pill for that - I can certainly tell you what not to do. I have made many of the mistakes in this book, therefore one of main goals it to help YOU avoid these same mistakes. Figure it out now, not in 10 years when your prospects for success have diminished.

Let's start with a basic test of where you are (and be truthful to yourself):

1. Do you understand what role you want to play in the music industry? If you are in a band, does each member of the band understand his or her role in the group?

2. Do you write and/or perform GREAT songs?

3. Have you created world-class sound recordings?

4. Do you have professional promotional materials?

5. Have you created an amazing live show?

6. Do you tour and showcase often?

7. Have you built an impactful online presence?

8. Have you learned how to deal with the media?

9. Do you treat your music career as a business?

10. Do you plan for your success?

11. Do you go after every possible revenue stream?

12. Are you prepared to work very hard for a sustained period of time?

You may be able to answer YES to a few of these, and that is great. The real trick is to be able to answer YES to all of the above questions. The music business is extremely competitive. If you are competing with artists who have dealt with all of the above 12 issues and you have not, then you have basically taken yourself out of the race. If you can honestly say that you have conquered all of these 12 areas, then you have given yourself a fighting chance to succeed.

Please note that all underlined words correspond to hyperlinks in the eBook version of this book. I have included all of these web links by chapter as an appendix to this book. The hyperlinks are also available as a companion to the printed book at:
http://www.adagiomusic.ca/a-career-in-music/.

Chapter 1 Understanding your role in the music industry

One fundamental mistake many artists make is to assume that there is only one way to achieve a career in the music business. Not everyone can be a rock star. There are many different paths one can take and various alternatives that compliment the work you do as an artist on stage. Also, keep in mind that in many cases it is not just one component that adds up to a career, but a combination of activities. Many artists must wear a number of hats to achieve a sustained career. It is very important to understand that the number of artists who achieve superstardom is miniscule. It is also a fact of life that the bulk of revenue in the business is actually earned by this same very small percentage of artists. This is not meant to discourage you, but to serve as a reality check.

Decide what you want to achieve and set your goals accordingly. If you are set on being the biggest artist in the world, then you must also be extremely motivated and driven. A good example of this is Nickelback. In the early 1990's, believe it or not, this band backed up my own band, Rymes with Orange – oh, how times have changed. The fact is, at that time, Nickelback was just another indie band in Vancouver, BC. As it turned out, the key to their success was Chad Kroeger's focus and drive. I recall years ago talking to Chad at the JUNO Awards after they had won many of the trophies. He seemed pre-occupied. When I questioned him about it, all he could talk about were problems they were having in Europe. He was at the JUNO Awards, but he was already planning his next big moves. Chad understood what he wanted to do and set out to achieve it. As a songwriter, he understood what radio wanted. As a performer, he understood what his audiences wanted. As a businessman, he understood what kind of commitment it would take to achieve the kind of success internationally that Nickelback has.

Ask yourself what you want to actually achieve in your career. It is OKAY to allow yourself to set your own path. Do you REALLY want to be like Justin Bieber, Nickelback, One Direction, Rihanna or Taylor Swift? Are you prepared to become part of a bigger machine or do you want to remain independent and enjoy the freedom to do whatever you want artistically?

I recently was told by one of the LA based music supervisors (a supervisor is a person whose job it is to place music on film, television, video games or commercials) for a major studio that her friend in a very hip independent label was bemoaning the fact that none of his artists were being played on the radio. The supervisor said, "Well, if you want to get your artists played on the radio, why don't you sign some artists who write radio songs?" It sounds funny, but it is very true. Radio is about selling advertising. The songs that they play have to appeal to a specific demographic so that those individuals in that demographic will listen to the radio. Listeners will hear advertising aimed at their demographic and advertisers will sell their products. If a song is played that does not appeal to that demographic and listeners turn to another station, then the station must pull it. Also, the advertising has to be slotted in during specific time periods, so 10-minute songs generally cannot be played. Unless the format of radio fundamentally changes, it is going to continue to be very difficult for artists who do not write "radio" songs to get on the radio. Further, with radio consolidation, the number of decision makers for play lists have shrunk to a very small number of people – all of whom are programming nationally. The small pipeline that is commercial radio has been shrunk even more.

Online promotion through YouTube, Twitter, Facebook, Bandcamp, Instagram and other services provides an alternate way to get known. An incredible example is Carly Rae Jepson. Two tweets from Justin Bieber led to her song "Call Me Maybe" becoming the biggest song in the world for a number of weeks in 2012. It launched her career. Interestingly, I have known Carly Rae as a local artist for 10 years. Her perceived over night success should be brought into perspective. Carly Rae made her own luck by hard work, dedication and talent. She had the goods. Unlike many fly-by-night artists online, she had the background and training to take advantage of the sudden global spike in online interest.

If you really, really want international success as a pop artist, then chances are you will make some significant artistic compromises and accept your position as a cog in the big machine that is the major label business. Of course, there is a lot of money to be made, but you have to be willing to live with both the upside and the downside of super success. You may become famous, but you will likely lose your privacy. You will travel the world constantly, but it will be very hard to maintain a "normal" family relationship. You will be fully employed and playing all the time, but no longer in charge of your schedule. As the old adage goes: be careful what you wish for.

In 1968 Andy Warhol said "in the future, everyone will be world-famous for 15 minutes." Is it the 15 minutes of fame that you are searching for? Or is it a career in the music business? Schmoyoho's Antoine Dodson "Hide the Kids,Hide the Wife" song had a huge viral success. Antoine got his 15 minutes of fame. Rebecca Black got her 15 minutes of fame from the "Friday" song. For the most part, the viral success stories are "novelty" acts and public interest is fleeting, as with these artist examples. In fact, the vast majority of top YouTube videos involve funny or controversial clips. Having said that, artists who are being noticed online are producing video productions that are compelling, exciting and creative. If you are more interested in a career in music than a mere 15 minutes of fame, consider making the kind of production that you will be proud of for years to come.

So, let's say that you accept that superstardom is a bit of a pipe dream given your creative interests. You play classical, jazz, folk, instrumental, art rock, progressive rock, alternative, indie or a variety of other non-mainstream music. That is your passion. That is what gets you up each morning. That is fine. That is good. Just don't get bitter if you do not achieve the kind of commercial success that you also want. My point is that you should understand your place in the world and embrace it. Focus on the activities that will actually help you move forward.

I learned a valuable lesson about roles early in my touring career. I played keyboards in a band called Rymes with Orange. One night after a particularly sweaty and fun show, I came off the stage and was extremely pumped. I went up to a group of fans to discuss the show.

The conversation went like this:

Bob: "So how did you like the show?"

Girl #1: "We loved it…what a blast." Boy #1: "So, who are you?"
Bob: "I am the keyboardist."
Girl #2: "There is a keyboard player in the band, really?"

Ouch… Unfortunately, there is a food chain with most bands. It often goes something like this:

1. Singer,
2. Guitarist,
3. Drummer,
4. Bass player,
5. Percussionist,
6. Sound man,
7. Merch person,
8. Bouncer and then,
9. Keyboardist (if keyboardist is also lead singer, then move up to #1)

All kidding aside, I learned to accept that my role was to support the other players. Once I made peace with that, life was much better.

My role as a musician and creator has evolved and changed and that is just fine with me. In the ambient instrumental duo Mythos I am an equal partner with the guitarist and in this role I am musician and producer, which has really allowed me to thrive. Additionally, over the past five years, I have spent time co-writing with other artists, which has given me yet a different role, and another set of skills to play out

Look into your heart and ask yourself what role you really want to play in the music business and, more importantly, what you are suited for. Are you truly a front person? Do you have that "it" factor? Are you a stand out or solo musician? Are you more comfortable in a supporting role? Perhaps you are even more comfortable with a behind the scenes role? Consider a hockey team. There are the stars, but there are also the grinders, the enforcers, the defenders, the coach, the trainers and unfortunately the owners and general managers. The analogy is uncannily close to the reality of the music business.

There are numerous other jobs in music: producer, manager, agent, songwriter, film composer and other creative and business positions. Many artists wear more than one of these hats simultaneously. It is part of the new DIY world. In addition, artists who have long-term careers in music learn the importance of adaptation. A good example of this is my former business partner and friend Marc LaFrance.

Marc tours internationally with Randy Bachman and Fred Turner (BTO/Guess Who). In the 1970s, he was an 'up and comer' in Winnipeg and as a vocalist, he had the potential to be the "next big thing". While management errors squashed his superstar dream, Marc went on in the 1980's to be one of the industry's top vocal session singers. He sang on Motley Crüe, Bon Jovi, Cher, AC/DC and many other records. He sang commercial jingles in the 80s, and recorded his own solo record – which is to this day a go-to album for 80s sounding tracks for film and TV. At the same time, Marc had his cover band "Cease and Desist" which played every kind of club and corporate gig you can imagine.

In the 90's, the studio work dried up and Marc started using the talents that he had developed building Cease and Desist to help other artists. During this period, there were a lot of international licensing deals around and Marc and I had incredible success working international conferences such as MIDEM for artists. We also found many film, television and video game placements for our clients. In the 2000's, the industry went into a tailspin. The labels started being very "safe". That meant focusing support on "know quantities" like The Eagles, The Police, AC/DC and the Guess Who.

Marc and his band mates in Cease and Desist eventually landed the gig touring the world with Randy Bachman and Fred Turner. In his later career, Marc was all of a sudden living the "rock star" life that he didn't get in his 20s. During all of this, Marc remained a vocal activist in favour of artist rights.

In Canada, he was part of a group that pushed for compensation for performers on recordings played on the radio ("Neighbouring Rights"). When this initiative was adopted into Canada, Marc suddenly started getting new royalties for all of the performances on records from the 1980s. Marc's story is an amazing one. He has made his living ENTIRELY from the music industry, but not without being willing to adapt to new environments. It is this kind of spirit that we can all learn from in trying to make our path through this very difficult industry.

The moral of this story is that CHANGE is the only guarantee in life. If you want to make a living in music, be ready to wear many hats and adapt to new opportunities and environments. Understand your role in the band and your position in the industry and embrace it. Your life will be far better once you do.

Chapter 2 Songwriting

Malcolm Gladwell's book <u>Outliers</u> proposes that mastery of a task requires at least 10,000 hours of practice. Many professional artists have mastered their instruments having already put in the years of practice. So what about songwriting? Although many artists are amazing at playing, they struggle with writing songs. That is because the craft of songwriting requires the same amount of practice that playing does. Just because you are a doctor, does not mean that you are a brain surgeon. Separate skill sets are required, and you must be willing to put in those same 10,000 hours for each skill.

So, now pretend you are a young band with a killer live show. I guarantee the number one complaint from the industry is going to be the songwriting. As an artist, you might feel the urge to resist all input from more experienced writers. You might fight your studio producer tooth and nail for every change that is suggested. You will likely want to protect your "artistic integrity". My advice is to help yourself and give in. Co-write with experienced writers; listen to experienced producers. There is an extremely good chance that you are a better player than a songwriter.

"It all starts with a song," sounds trite. It is said so often that it is hard to even write down. But, it is true nonetheless. There is a big difference between a "good" song and a "great" song. A "good" song can become a "great" song, but much of this is a question of the artistic process: digging and digging, re-writing, pulling your hair out, and doing it all over again. Sure, there is that occasional song that seems to write itself and come out of nowhere, but they are few and far between.

My theory on songs arising as magic from the ether is that the more songwriting you do, the more stimulation you provide to the creative part of your brain. And soon, you start to notice this creativity flowing even when you are not writing. Your sub-conscious is constantly working when you are in this state. I have experienced the "song that wrote itself", but that was when I was writing an album and had written probably 10 crappy songs. The point is that all veteran songwriters say the same thing: you need to write every day. Just like you practice your instrument every day, you need to flex that songwriting muscle, and don't forget those 10,000 hours.

Another phenomenon that many artists experience is that they feel their latest song is by far their best song. I understand that you are excited about your new music, but objectively that does not necessarily mean it is your best. Do not be afraid to pull from your catalogue. Tom Cochrane had a demo of a song sitting on a cassette called "Love is a Highway". Before the album, this song was reviewed by the production team along with many of Tom's other archived songs. The song didn't happen until one of his band mates suggested the title "Life is a Highway." This set off a spark and Tom went off and wrote the biggest song of his career.

One songwriting tip that flows from Tom Cochrane's example is to start with a title. In other words, start from your main chorus and write back from there. Like any map, it is always a good idea to know what your destination is. "Life is a Highway" was written from the chorus hook back and it certainly worked.

Further to the point of titles, some bands find it cool to name songs in a way that has little to do with the song itself. If you want the song on the radio, I suggest naming the song from your chorus. Sometimes trying to be too cool can backfire. If someone phones in a request, how is the DJ going to know how to match the fans description of the song with the song itself? Fans will often simply ask for the words in the chorus when they don't know the song title.

Record everything. That does not mean that you should create finished master recordings of every song that you write. Many new artists blow their precious funding getting talked into recording their unfinished songs at a master level. The term "you can't polish a turd" applies very well here. Now just because Myth Busters proved that you can, in fact, polish a turd (and personally I think that some big pop artists have managed to do so), that doesn't mean you should try to do that. You will spend a lot of money and end up with a stinker.

My Advice: Record 20 songs in a rough way, work with a song doctor or a producer to pick the best three and record those really well. Your dad or uncle's funding is probably a one-timer. Waste it at your peril.

As music consultants and business professionals, we often run into a brick wall when trying to advise artists on their songwriting. If we start talking about "hooks" and "song structure" eyes start to roll. I have heard once or twice before, "Dude, we are artists and write what we feel. We don't want to write for radio. Radio should change to play us, because we rock." These may be noble thoughts, but they are not very practical.

I challenge any songwriter to consider their favorite songs of all time. What are the songs that inspire you? What are the songs that continue to stay in your playlists? What songs do you go back to time and time again because they make you smile or take you to another place? These are the "great" songs. Surely, you want to write one of those? If you do, consider the following observations about "great" songs:

a.   Every great song has a melody that distinguishes it from all other songs. Think of Mozart's "Eine Kleine Nachtmusik" Allegro written in 1787. I imagine that most people who know any music would know this melody:

It is so well known that any school child could finish the musical phrase started by the first two bars of music. Undeniable, memorable, hundreds of years old and still alive and well.

b.   Every great song has something in it that is incredibly memorable. Yes this can be the main chorus melody, but this can also be parts like Keith Richard's opening guitar chords for "Start Me Up", Phil Collin's tom fills in "In the Air Tonight", Jimmy Pages's guitar passages in "Stairway to Heaven" and the list goes on. Call it a "hook" or call it "something you remember", but every great song has something that is undeniably special.

c.   MOST great modern songs have a chorus. OK, some great songs have a "refrain" like "Bridge over troubled water". However, besides Bob Dylan and other eminent storyteller songwriters, the verses of a song have to lead somewhere – usually to a chorus. "All Verse" songs are often very dissatisfying, unless their lyrics are deeply profound and compelling. If you write a chorus, you are not selling out. You are recognizing that "song form" exists for a reason. Verses set up the chorus. (Bridges are a great addition and I personally love a good bridge, but a chorus is essential).

d.   MOST great songs are re-written and re-worked before they are finally recorded. Harry Shaw, in Errors in English and Ways to Correct Them (HarperCollins) says, "There is no such thing as good writing. There is only good rewriting." This applies to songwriting in a big way. One of the key mistakes made by songwriters is to give up on a song before it is truly ready to record. If someone tells you that a song dropped from the sky fully written, the chances are that some changes were made after the initial inspiration. Many, many songs started as "good" and only made it to "great" by re-writing.

e.   MOST great songs are written by songwriters who have written many other songs. Songwriting develops certain brain activity that builds on itself and enhances the creative process. It is like turning a faucet on. Once flowing, the water flows a lot easier. Great songwriters write all the time and never stop improving their craft.

f.   Lyric writing is an art unto itself. Bernie Taupin writes all of Elton John's lyrics. Elton John is a masterful instrumentalist and singer. He also writes amazing melodies and music. He is however, not a lyricist, which we found out really quickly when he tried to do it himself!

g.   Keep in mind that lyrics can be a vehicle for melody. I witnessed this in Europe when I saw kids singing to songs phonetically, in languages they did not understand. How the words interact melodically, sonically, phonetically, and poetically are all extremely important considerations.

Another must is to analyze every Beatles song that you can. As far as song craft goes, it is difficult to find a better "university" to study melody, song structure and lyrics.

There are lots of great resources to help songwriters. SOCAN, The Songwriter's Association of Canada SAC, and provincial music industry associations all put on workshops and seminars. Attend them! For a portal to all of the provincial music industry associations, please go to the Canadian Council of Music Industry Associations CCMIA.

Co-write! Let yourself grow as a songwriter. Don't hold on so tight that you smother your creation. Co-writing is an amazing thing. While it is not for everyone, I believe that every songwriter should certainly try it. Even if the songs do not get cut, the shared knowledge and extra tools that you can add to your toolbox are amazing. There is also something great when you are able to bounce ideas back and forth. The easiest co-write situation is two people, but three or four can work if everyone is respectful of each other.

I have learned a great deal from co-writing with other writers. For example, I have written with Shaun Verreault from Wide Mouth Mason. Shaun has a wonderful way of writing lyrics. He keeps a notebook that allows him to capture a constant free-flow of consciousness – he writes on every line, front and back of the page. On one occasion, when we were stuck in our writing process, he suddenly picked up his notebook, frantically leafed through it and pointed to a line buried deep in the middle pages. It was the perfect line. This resource, and his seemingly endless tool chest of guitar chops, makes writing with Shaun a joy. Finding good writing partners can be a bit of trial and error. No matter what, though, co-writing will help you develop as a songwriter.

Many bands are co-writing partnerships as well as performers. This can be great when it works, but can also be a disaster waiting to happen. In my old band, there were literally fistfights over song parts. We had one rehearsal that lasted less than a minute when the drummer launched himself over the drums to go after the guitarist because of a songwriting dispute. Everyone was constantly battling to get their ideas into songs. Contention can sometimes lead to some great material, but it can be a painful way to write. In some cases, it has nothing to do with songwriting, but the split of money that would come from the songwriting credits. Ironically, bands are often fighting over pennies in reality. My advice is to let the songwriters in the band be the songwriters. The band can always agree to have some publishing revenue go to the band and that revenue can be split between the band members. This creates a "safety valve" and can also make the creative process less combative.

This chapter in no way is meant to be a "how to" on songwriting. It represents some of my observations over the years. There are many great books that have been written to help songwriters develop their craft and I encourage you to read them all. As a start, go to:

Murphy's Laws of Songwriting: The Book - by Ralph Murphy (Ralph also works for ASCAP in the USA and attends a lot of their conferences. He is an amazingly warm and helpful man and literally has one degree of separation from most of the key people in the music industry).

How to Write a Hit Song - by Molly-Ann Leiken.

Writing Better Lyrics - by Pat Pattison.

Melody in Songwriting: Tools and Techniques for Writing Hit Songs (Berklee Guide) - by Jack Perricone.

The Craft and Business of Songwriting - by John Braheny.

Songwriters on Songwriting - by Paul Zollo.

The Craft of Lyric Writing - by Sheila Davis.

6 Steps To Songwriting Success: Comprehensive Guide To Writing And Marketing Hit Songs - by Jason Blume.

The Songwriters Idea Book: 40 Strategies to Excite Your Imagination, Help You Design Distinctive Songs, and Keep Your Creative Flow - by Sheila Davis.

Chapter 3 Creating world-class sound recordings

Recording is completely different than live performance. When you make a mistake live it is gone as soon as it happens, but in the studio a mistake can last forever (which actually can be a good thing in some circumstances). This creates a kind of pressure on recorded performance that can make studio work very intense. It can take a long time to get comfortable in the recording environment.

Performing live affords room to breathe and expand on parts. Recording means crystallizing and distilling your songs into well-crafted representations of your art. This means spending a lot of time in pre-production before you enter the studio. Pre-production is the time when you really need to think about which songs are going to make the cut, how the songs are going to be arranged and recorded, and what instrumentation is going to be used. Production is when it should all come together. Don't count on being able to just show up and make magic. Set the stage right so that the magic can happen.

I love the recording process, but to get it right, you need infinite patience, especially when dealing with technology. It can be frustrating at times when creativity is slowed down by the mechanics of recording – getting the right mike placement, making sure that levels are correct, having to do one part over and over until it is perfect. Try and get yourself into a good place. Create a comfortable environment to create in. You are probably going to be in the studio for some time and need to feel good in the space.

Studio

Everyone has a studio. Every computer can be easily turned into a recording platform. A good mike, pre-amp and interface, and ProTools or Logic is all you need and off you go. Sounds too good to be true, right? Well, everything has a catch. Today, it is not about the equipment so much, as it is about the producer. Most producers worth their salt have access to enough gear to record and mix a world-class record. Remember the 10,000 hours rule? Well this applies to producing as well. Of course, I encourage you to learn everything you can about production and engineering, but don't forget that producing a recording that will stand up against every other track in the world takes real dedication.

What studio do you need? Your genre will undoubtedly dictate how big a studio you require. If you are a full production rock band, you will need a big studio for the drums and maybe the guitars. If you are a singer-songwriter with guitar/vocal and limited overdubs, everything can be recorded in a smaller project studio. If you are a pop band, access to amazing drum, bass and keyboard sample libraries is critical. If you are a chamber orchestra, you will need a very specialized facility with an engineer who understands the subtleties of miking multiple acoustic instruments. Costs will vary widely from project to project.

Producer

Choosing a producer. As far as choosing a producer goes, this is an extremely important artist decision. While one producer may be ideal for one artist, it does not mean that the same producer is best suited for you. Spend a lot of time on this. If you have the luxury of trying one song with a producer to see if the chemistry is there, do that.

Understand the difference between a good producer and a good engineer. There are a lot of amazing engineers who fancy themselves producers, but are really not. An engineer has the technical training to get great sounds for you. A producer, on the other hand, gets involved with song doctoring, song arrangement, instrumental and vocal part choices, creative decisions as well as budgets, studio booking and a variety of other functions. The confusion is that there are some amazing producer/engineers who share both technical proficiency and can dive into the songs from a creative standpoint. Use this test to tell the difference: If the "producer" does not want to do pre-production, and says something to you like, "Just come in and we will lay the tracks down…" this is a good sign that they are not a producer. Pre-production is the time before you step foot in the studio in order to get the songs ready for recording. This means demoing all of your songs in a rough way, having the producer listen to your songs and choosing the ones that show the most promise. Pre-production entails digging down into the songs, tearing them apart and building them back up. This is a time when a lot of artists really dig their heals in and when the most amount of tension with producers can arise.

My advice: Let the process happen. Let go a bit. If you feel the urge to protect your songs like a mother bear, resist that temptation. This is a place where good songs can turn into great songs.

Once the songs are well rehearsed and ready to record, it is time to head into the studio. When you start spending money, this is the time to know exactly what you want to do. Don't waste time in an expensive studio writing parts. That should have all been done before you arrive. Of course, you want to leave room for "happy mistakes", but those will come through the process.

Working in a studio with a really good producer and engineer can be an amazing education. As the keyboardist in Rymes with Orange, I observed everything that the producers and engineers would allow me to. I watched them set up the mikes, EQ, set up the pre-amps, record and mix. I was able to learn how to get the best sound from mike placement and room sound, and decipher between a "good take" and a "bad take". I was told that you tape EVERYTHING because you never know when you are going to get an amazing take. I learned to record the first take, because sometimes that is the best take you will ever get. There is so much knowledge to gain from these pros and you can use these skills for doing your own pre-production and writing in the future.

For me, finding success as the producer and artist for the group Mythos would not have happened without many hours spent learning from the best. If you log enough hours recording and mixing, maybe you will become a producer too. Daniel Lanois and Trevor Horn are all both accomplished musicians who turned to producing. Ryan Guldemond from Mother Mother is not only a great frontman, he is also an amazing producer for other artists. You may find that production becomes your long-term "role" in the business.

Mixing Engineer

Stand-alone mixing engineers have become a very important addition to the process. A great mixing engineer can bring your project to an entirely new level. I found this out early on when producer Bill Buckingham mixed our first Rymes with Orange record "Peel". He blew us away. In one instance, he taught me the power of silence in music. He added a global mute to a key part of the track that actually made the song eminently more impactful. We were able to incorporate that break into our live set to create a really amazing "moment".

I have seen what mixing engineers like Mike Fraser (AC/DC) or Randy Staub (Nickelback) can do for a track. It is incredible. The advantage of using a separate mixing engineer is that they have "fresh ears". They come into the process with an unbiased opinion. I have yet to see a great mixing engineer take away from the production process.

Mastering

Mastering is another stage in the process that is very important. Mastering is the process whereby the final mixes are prepared for commercial release. This is not the time to scrimp and save. Great mastering is the icing on the cake, it can put the finishing coat of polish on the project. If done badly, it can also completely ruin all the work that you have done. A great mastering house will not change the mix, it will simply ensure that the mixes are optimally EQed, compressed and expanded, ready for radio and final release.

Artist as producer. Many artists want to be the producer as well as the artist. Often this is simply an ego thing. Without disrespecting producers who I hold in great esteem, the average fan could not tell you who produced a record. Fans care about the artist. Let the producer do their job and make your tracks come alive. If you have chosen the right producer, he or she will help you to get to the next level in your development.

Don't chase a trend. A great song can be produced any number of ways and can even cross genre barriers. When deciding how to record your music I think that it is important to follow your heart not your head. What I mean by this is that if you are too worried about the "market" and the current "trends", then you may be setting yourself up for failure. If you are chasing a trend, then you are probably too late to take advantage of that trend. By the time you actually release your music, the fickle music world will have moved on to another fad. I suggest that you decide who you are and what you are and be the best at that. Don't try to emulate some other band.

I really learned this lesson with Mythos. When I was playing in rock bands, my band mates were often obsessed with the sounds and influences of the time. All of our production had to emulate those trends. I remember actually changing the sound of songs because they did not match the current beats and instrumentations of the time. This is a game that ultimately leads to (a) dating your music, and (b) making sure that you are lumped in with a trend and not considered truly original.

When Paul Schmidt and I started Mythos, this was for me in response to my soul-destroying experiences as a rock musician. I felt beaten up by the business and wanted to return to why I wanted to be a musician in the first place. The only criterion that Paul and I set was to create beautiful music (I realize that sounds corny, but it is the truth). We did not worry about trends, genres or musical borders. Having said that, we did create music with form and substance, but we did not worry so much about making money. The result: the most commercially successful musical project of my career. We released our sixth record in fifteen years, we have won awards, we have charted on Billboard and our sales are in the six figures. We found a niche in the ambient instrumental world. I think that the reason that we have been so successful is that we put creation first.

Does this seem to contradict what I was saying earlier about songwriting and radio? Not really. Most music created is not destined for commercial radio. It is a question of accepting where you fit in the music business world, embracing that and being the best in your chosen area. Like Mythos, you may not be creating music that will be played on commercial radio. The beauty is that, with the internet, you do not have to be something you are not. There is a place for every kind of music online. You simply need to reach out and find your fans.

At the end of the day, creating recorded music that sets you apart from every other artist on the planet should be your main aim. This may seem like a lofty goal, but if you want to make your mark, you have to find something that distinguishes you from everyone else. You will probably find that in your creative heart, not in your intellectual head.

Chapter 4 Professional Promotional Materials

A great way to turn off anyone in the industry is to present amateur promotional materials. If even one element is off, then the individuals who can actually make a difference in your career will assume that you are not ready or not serious enough. This goes for labels, publishers, managers, agents, funders, radio, television – you name it.

Why would you spend a great deal of time perfecting your instrument craft, your songwriting, and your recording and then supplement that with a terrible website, lame picture, poorly written bio, and no videos? Why sell yourself short? I hate to pick on jazz and classical musicians, but I have been shocked by the state of the materials in the promo packages I have received. This is particularly disheartening because, often these musicians have practiced 5 hours a day for 20 years and recorded incredible performances. A distinct exception to this is a jazz band called "Metalwood". They understood effective marketing and built a brand that really stood out in their genre. This helped them to get noticed and certainly pushed them forward in their path to winning numerous JUNO Awards. Anna Netrebko is a great example of a classical artist who has transcended the normal boundaries of classical music recognition. Have a look at how these artists have created an image and cultivated their brand. The point here is that it doesn't matter what genre you are in, the same principals apply.

Let's take a step back. What promo materials should all artists have?:

a.   **Professional Picture.** This is not necessarily about spending a lot of money, but you can if you want. Great photographers are not cheap, but it could be a great investment in your career. If you are on a budget, then find a student photographer who has great talent. No matter what you decide to do, consider the following:

    i.   what kind of image will perfectly capture your band?,
    ii.   what should the band wear? (pros often have stylists who can get all sorts of cool demo cloths), and
    iii.   where are you going to shoot (indoors or out)?
    iv.   Some tips:

        A.   do not take a picture against a brick wall or on a railway track,
        B.   Do not be so "artsy" the picture is not clear and out of focus,
        C.   take both black & white and colour pictures – newspapers and magazines will need both options,
        D.   make sure that you have high resolution versions of all of your pictures in digital form, and
        E.   choose the best shot and stay with it for a while (this will help define your image).

Some bands have gone with shots that are blurry, do not show their faces or they even wear masks. This may be part of your overall marketing strategy, but keep in mind that some people in the industry or in the media might just get turned off. If you are OK with that, then fine. Just know what impact your decisions make on possible success.

b. **Biography.** Wow, I have read some bad bios full of typos, spelling mistakes, bad grammar, cockiness and even profanity. Bands often think that they are being "cool" by being offensive. This cannot be farther from the truth. Now, if you are a punk band and don't give a crap about what the "man" thinks, then maybe the anti-bio will work for you, but for most artists a well written bio can really help to move their career forward.

A good bio tells a story – your story – in a way that compels the reader to want to read on. In the best case, the press will simply lift parts of your bio out and use that for their article. Bios should tell the reader who you are, where you are from, what motivated you to become a musician, what you have done (awards, records, tours, charts, etc.). Early in your career, your bio will be less about your achievements and more about your goals. Don't BS and do not over-exaggerate. People in the business know each other and know if you are lying about your track record.

Accept where you are in your career and write from that perspective. Never be afraid of who you are and where you come from. It is OK to be from a small town or a big city.

c. **Amazing Demos.** Less is more! It is better to have fewer songs available that are killer than a lot of weak tracks. Always put your best foot forward. Some bands will put their best and/or most accessible songs last. Don't do that, as the listener may never get to the last song. The first song has to knock them out.

d. **Compelling Video content.** We live in a YouTube world, so you need content. It is a fact of life now. This does not mean MTV style big production videos, it means really creative, well thought out videos. Said the Whale "We are 1980" is a great example of a video shot from a modest budget with a really, really cool concept. Dominique Fricot "HauntedbyLove" is another example. These videos look great, and sound great, but most importantly they have a huge amount of creative soul.

e. **Complete and current website.** All of your promotional materials MUST be readily available online – your hi-res pics, your bio, your music and links to your videos. The first thing that anyone in the industry does is check out your website. If they don't have your URL, they will Google you. I can't emphasize how important it is to have professional promotional materials presented on an easily accessible and useful website. Don't use flash! Apple does not use flash and you cannot cut and paste from it. Flash based sites are very annoying to anyone in the industry.

Branding

An over-riding consideration is "branding". With your name and image, you are creating a brand that needs to be consistent and developed over time. When designing your promotional materials, make sure that every element matches your brand – even the font is a consideration. Developing a logo is a great idea. This can become your calling card – something to put on backdrops, drum skins, T-shirts. In fact, coming up with a logo as a representation of your name is very important. Some bands also have a symbol and a name logo to represent the band. The Rolling Stones red lips and tongue are immediately recognized as their trademark.

Your promotional materials as well as your merchandise all need to be an expression of your brand. If you nurture your image, over time this could become the most valuable property that you have. Gene Simmons is likely the undisputed king of the brand with "KISS". This brand is worth tens of millions of dollars. Now, I am not saying that you have to be as overly crass as KISS, but at least recognize how important the brand is. "D.O.A." is a brand, however if you had asked the band back in the day if they thought that there would be value in their name, they probably would have spit on you - literally. Branding was never what the punk movement was about. So, finding the balance between being true to your art and cultivating your brand can be tricky. Only you can know how "commercial" you want to push the brand. Think about what kind of merchandise ("merch") fits your image. Be creative. The same principal applies to merch as your CDs. Fans want to take something away that will remind them of the experience you gave them.

Chapter 5 Creating a killer live show

Tom Jackson is a live performance producer from Nashville who was instrumental in building Taylor Swift's live performance. I have worked with him on many occasions and never fail to learn something new every time I see him do a live critique or a seminar. Many new artists who are told about Tom and people like Tom shy away for a number of reasons:

  a.   It isn't "cool" to produce a live show,
  b.   producing a show takes away from the spontaneity of the performance,
  c.   we are a rock band and don't want to look like a Vegas show, or
  d.   our fans love what we do already.

There are many more excuses, but the bottom line is that the separation of "good" performers from "great" performers is grounded in the little things. With any resource, you need to take out what is useful for you. Read Tom Jackson's Live Music Method book. Watch his DVDs. Normally, I would not single out one source, but for some reason, there are very few people doing what Tom is doing. We need more people getting involved in live performance production in the same way that we have with record production.

Some key messages that I learned from Tom:

  a.   **People hear with their eyes.** This may seem counter-intuitive, but it is so true. If a vocalist is on a mike and singing, people are naturally drawn to that vocalist. If the vocalist steps back even a step and the guitarist who is about to solo steps up, eyes are drawn to the right place. It seems simple, but so many bands stand in one spot and do nothing.

  b.   **If you look the same, you sound the same.** Bands often rely on the fact that their songs are different to try and create a varied set, but they do not change how they look on stage. You need to consider that the "pressure" on the audience needs to change throughout a set. Sets often look like a stew (Tom calls it goulash) rather than a fine meal. Bands often "get off" bouncing around the stage all the time. The audience just sees a mess and it is confusing. If thought is put into where everyone should be, then it frees each member to focus on his or her role within the band.

  c.   **If you create moments, you will create fans.** Fans want to be moved, they want to be touched emotionally and for their lives to be changed. That is why they go to concerts. If you can achieve that in a fan, you will have a fan for life. If a fan comes out of a gig feeling let down, the opposite is true. If you create a "moment" for a fan, they will want to remember that experience, so they will buy your merch and CDs.

I work with many bands that think "producing" their show is contrary to their independent spirit; that thinking about creating a proper live event takes away from their freedom and spontaneity. The truth is that at some point they will have to up their game to move forward. To me, it is simply the difference between a professional and an amateur.

Many bands get caught in the bar circuit and get frustrated as to why they do not progress to bigger venues. I always like to say that you should understand the room that you are playing in, but always be busting out of the room. If you are playing a 400 capacity venue, you should be thinking about playing the 1000 seater. If you do that, there is a better chance that a promoter or agent will think that you are ready to progress.

Never, ever phone in a concert. There are many stories of bands that played to a handful of people and got significant industry interest from their performance. I remember years ago seeing Sloan play in the Commodore Ballroom in Vancouver during the old Music West conference – there were only ten people in the audience! However, as it turns out, all ten of them were major label A&R guys. Sloan played their hearts out and they were signed shortly after that show. If you are playing to an empty room, you are actually auditioning for the owner, the bartender, and the staff. Also, there are tastemakers in every community; people who have the ear of their peers. If they hear you and like you, they will tell their friends. I can guarantee that if you kick ass for the room, the next time you are there, word of mouth will ensure a bigger audience. If you continue to do that, you will build a loyal fan base. *You never know who is in the room.*

Break your show down and build it back up. You need to consider the audience in designing a show. Song order, for example, is very important. You should always end with a bang, usually your most popular song. Don't save that for an encore – you might not get one. Having said that, always have a great encore ready to go. As far as the flow of the set, make sure to figure out the best way to keep your audience engaged from song to song. Remember that there are different levels of pressure the audience will feel. If you play an entire set of heavy songs with no rest, the audience may feel exhausted. If you play a whole set of ballads, the audience may be sleeping by the end of your show. Once you have a good set list worked out, remember that the same issue of "pressure" applies to each song. You can think about how each song should look and feel as well. Ask yourself how you can keep the audience interested and engaged throughout each song. Songs played live can and should be altered to work in that environment. Allow your songs to breathe in the live environment. Work on your transitions, your banter, when you are going to tune, whether you are using any props, where everyone needs to be during each song (so you are not bumping into each other).

Just because you are getting off on a song, does not mean that the audience is. A lot of bands make the mistake of thinking that if they are having a great time bouncing around the stage, the audience is feeling the same way. Young bands might spend a significant amount of time facing the drummer. That is a natural thing to do if you rehearse in a small room. The "comfort zone" for bands that rehearse in a circle is to look at each other. This is the opposite of what an audience needs. The best way to practice your live show is on a stage similar to the ones you expect to play on during your tour.

The best-case scenario is to rehearse with your soundman so that you can integrate FX and other production needs into your set – but we can't always afford that luxury. When I first started touring, our band was quite green; it took about 10 shows to get a good show hobbled together. As to why we did not work this all out before we left? I am sure the audiences in our first 10 shows were thinking the same thing.

Always try and improve and you will continue to play to bigger audiences. I like the example of Coldplay. I OD'd on them in the early part of the 2000s. When I first saw Chris Martin live, I was disappointed. He seemed uncomfortable and jerky. He looked at his feet a lot and did not communicate very well with the audience. Thank goodness his voice was amazing, or I might not have come back. The second time I saw the band, it was clear he had worked on his stage presence and the band as a whole performed a better show. I came away feeling much more satisfied about my beliefs in the band. Last year I went to the "Mylo Xyloto" tour and was simply blown away. The band grew from a cool, trippy rock band to being on par with U2. This wasn't a concert: it was an event, something to talk about and remember. It was exciting. Chris had grown into a true frontman. I will be a fan for life now. It doesn't matter who you are, you can always grow as an artist.

Your live show is going to sustain you through your career. It is going to earn you the bulk of your revenue. Make sure that you spend a great deal of time, effort and attention to developing an entertaining and professional show.

Chapter 6 Touring and Showcasing

Touring is a big part of finding success as a recording artist. If you and your band are not interested in touring, it might be best to look for a different path in the music industry. The days of the television based MTV or MuchMusic videos breaking an artist are long gone. More importantly, artists make over 90% of their income from live performance revenues. This is not a new thing, but now more than ever, if you want a career as a recording artist, you have to be on the road.

John Naisbitt wrote a visionary book that talks about human interaction with technology. His basic view is that technology is important, but it is the interaction of "High Tech, High Touch" that is the new paradigm. In order to be truly effective in the new digital world that we live in you need to take advantage of high tech such as the internet, but never forget that it is the direct individual human connection that will win the day.

This interaction between technology and human contact applies very well to the music business. Online presence is essential, but live performance is even more relevant than ever. It is the place where you connect with your fans. It is the place where you can actually sell CDs and merchandise. It is the place where your fans will truly fall in love with you. Now, combine your live presence with social media and you can create a very powerful and successful plan to propel your career forward.

Only ten years ago, the basic record sales model was still viable. Record Labels would fund sound recordings, videos and tour support in order to drive sales of CDs. That model is all but dead. Now, any CDs out there have become merch items to be sold at gigs. While artists used to tour to support records for labels, artists now tour to make their living and CDs are a way to allow people to take home the experience.

The number one question asked at Music BC (BC's music industry association) after "how do I get a manager?" is "how do I get an agent?" The short answer is that getting an agent is easy once your guarantees are over $1000+ per show. The bottom line is that agents make 10% of your gross revenues from shows. You may not be attractive to an agent if you are being paid $100 and a case of beer. Build your fan base and the agents will come.

One great way to find venue spots is the app, Tourhub. This is a service developed by the CCMIA for anyone to use, free of charge. Tourhub is a venue database and touring tool that allows you to search for venues across Canada and obtain contact information. The app also allows you to confirm and plot the dates, map the tour out, advance gigs and build a merch inventory. Any new venues added by other artists are automatically added to the database for you to access

If you haven't toured before, start modestly. Do 4-5 dates in and around your home town. Then try a provincial tour. Then, a regional tour. Then, a national tour (hopefully with a conference/festival anchor showcase). Touring is expensive and it's likely you will lose money on the first few tours. The hope is that the more you tour, the more you will build your fan base. Think of it as an investment in your career that will pay dividends in the future.

Managing merchandise. Remember that the principal way that you are going to make money before your live performance revenues generate more than a break even is your merch sales. Resist the temptation to give too much merch away. T-shirts are much more expensive than CDs to manufacture. Consider giving away a sticker or a CD before an expensive merch item. A poignant example stands out for me. During a tour I was managing, the band played the COCA Conference to get gigs in colleges around Canada. One night at an after party, I was exhausted and went to have a nap in the van. While I was sleeping, the band raided the trailer and gave away about $4,000 worth of T-Shirts to all of the college students at the party. The idea was to get the students excited about the band, but it took a long time for us to recover financially. The point is that you have to know when to give and when to sell. Consider selling to venue staff at cost or allocating only a certain amount of items to be 'giveaways'. Keep an accurate log of all inventory and sales.

Financing merchandise. Labels will often help finance a band's merch. The regular deal is they keep 50% of net revenues for providing the inventory. This is a pretty high share of revenue, so if you can finance the merch yourself, this is a good way to go. There are also companies and investors who specialize in financing merch, but their deals are usually 50% of net revenue as well. It is a question as to whether you can afford to finance the inventory.

Showcasing at big conferences is often seen as a "waste of time". Artists think, "there are too many artists and too much competition for industry eyeballs." While there can be some truth in that, there is a flip side to the equation. Getting accepted at key showcase events such as SXSW (USA), CMJ (USA), Reeperbahn (Germany), Folk Alliance (North America), CMW (Canada), Big Sound (Australia), BreakOut West (Canada), ECMA (Canada), M for Montreal (Canada) and The Great Escape (UK) can open a lot of doors for artists. Furthermore, it separates you from the pack. Merely being chosen to attend a major showcase is a very big vote of confidence. Also, while in attendance there are always opportunities to network with buyers and possible partners. I consider showcasing a part of a bigger plan to build your career.

If you do showcase at a major conference, festival or awards show make sure that you spend the time to get as many industry people as possible out to your show. If they do not attend your show, do not despair. You can get a "buzz" going at a conference through word of mouth that ensures industry will make a point of seeing you the next time you are in town. Another event strategy is to make sure that you get more than one showcase. One of the biggest problems is that industry members have a list of artists that they want to see, but often have schedule conflicts. If you are able to give them two or three options, then you have a far better chance of getting seen. If you cannot get a second official showcase, look at trying to get onto an industry association showcase or a showcase at another event that someone other than the festival organizer has control over. Do your homework about events. Some are better than others. Bigger does not always mean better. For example, BreakOut West is a conference and festival with a much smaller scale than something like CMW or SXSW. At these big events, you are likely a small fish in a big pond. At the smaller events, you may have more access to industry and also have a better chance of being seen.

Some provinces have showcase opportunities, like Pacific Contact in BC or Contact East in Atlantic Canada. These are conferences where "buyers" source artists to book at their venues throughout their territories. CMJ in New York is an amazing place to source out US based college radio and campus touring.

Touring is of critical importance in today's new music industry paradigm. Touring is not only your most important promotional tool, it will eventually be the principal basis for your income. Start early and be ready to pay your dues. Also, keep in mind that every new territory that you try and conquer will mean starting the development process again. Many bands find it very difficult to take a step back from the success that they have had in Canada to play for smaller venues in the USA, Europe, Australia or Asia.

Once you have established a great live following and receive steady revenue from ticket sales, you will probably be hearing from one or all of these great Canadian agencies:

The Feldman Agency

The Agency Group

Paquin Entertainment

Chapter 7 Create an amazing online presence

The introduction of Johannes Gutenberg's printing press in 1450 was undoubtedly a turning point in human history. In generations to come, the introduction of the internet to modern society will probably be viewed in the same way. We live in a different world than we did even 15 years ago. It is exciting, but also scary and unpredictable. Music was one of the first media to be effected by the internet. Napster started the free download phenomenon and in one form or another this trend has lead to the collapse of the traditional record sales model. Digital sales through platforms such as iTunes have increased sales dramatically, but certainly not enough to compensate for the loss in physical sales. Record stores like Virgin, HMV, A&B Sound, Sam the Record Man, Tower Records and many others have simply closed stores or gone out of business. The dial is now moving even further away from the traditional music business model with the proliferation of "all you can eat" sites such as Spotify, Pandora and Rdio – one monthly fee allows streaming access to nearly every song ever recorded. Revenues from these streaming services are even lower than the paid download sites. Of these three, only Rdio is available in Canada.

We are right in the middle of a fundamental paradigm shift in the way that the public consumes music. People are discovering music in very different ways. Currently, the number one way for the world to discover new music is YouTube. That could change next week, but for now that is the way it is happening. Such sites as Facebook and Twitter are social media leaders, but as we saw with the rise and fall of MySpace, trends can leave as fast as they come. Many of us spend years building fan bases on MySpace only to find that the platform lost favour with the public.

HAVE YOUR OWN WEB SITE. As an artist, what do you need to have? You MUST have your own URL and website. This is of fundamental importance. This allows YOU to control content, sell from your store and most importantly collect your fan information directly.

Right now, Mark Zuckerberg and his partners at Facebook have control of all of your "friend" and "page like" data. Should Facebook shut down tomorrow, all of the contacts to your fans disappear. Data sourced through your website is critical to building a proper fan database. Fan email, Twitter handle, Facebook username and any other contact information that you can get from your fans should be gathered to ensure that there is always some way to get hold of them. Your fan data is worth its weight in gold.

If you can get one extra piece of information about a fan it would be where they live. That allows you to target market when you are touring. If you can get deeper information, like snail mail address, age or sex, great, but many people are simply not willing to give that up.

What should be on your website?

Consider your website as a portal to everything about you as an artist. It should be useful not only for fans, but also for the industry. It should be easy to navigate. Do not use flash or other proprietary systems. Use tools like WordPress to design the site. Easy to use, easy to access and designed for the lowest common denominator. Your website is where you put those world-class promotional materials to the test. It is the place where you want your fans and the industry to go. Most people will simply Google your band or artist name and expect the official band or artist website to pop up immediately. Make sure that you "optimize" your site with search engines. Your website designer can help you with this. If you are designing your own website, make sure that you register your site with all major search engines, especially Google.

Your website needs to have some basic elements and these elements must be integrated with your social media. The following should be easily accessible from the front page (home page) of your website. Some of these can be tabs at the top of your home page that link to separate sub-pages on your website. The essential website elements are as follows:

a. **Bio.** A great telling of your story is important. Make sure that you have a full biography available. This bio should be easily captured by "cut and paste" program functions. No flash design! You want people to get your story out there exactly the way that you are telling it.

b. **Pictures.** Hi-res pictures in both black and white and colour are essential. Newspapers, Magazines and other media need the choice. It would be a shame to be offered a colour feature in a newspaper and not have the colour picture to give to the reporter.

    If you want to protect your hi-res pictures, then you may want to consider a hidden press page on your web site. My opinion is keep things simple and easy for all users. Reporters rarely have the time to mess around with logins and passwords.

    Don't give a lot of choice for your press shots. As part of your branding, you want to give consistent imaging in the press everywhere you go.

c. **Music.** This is an interesting one. There are a plethora of music players that can be integrated into your site. The question is whether or not to allow downloading, streaming or a combination of the two. Only you can decide if you want to give your music away for free. The reality is that early on in your career, giving away music may be a good way to get fans and industry interested. There will come a point, however, when you will want to see a return on your significant recording investment. I suggest allowing one or two free downloads per album at the most. Stream everything. Do not stream partial songs. Fans and the industry alike really dislike that.

d. **Video**. As mentioned earlier, video content is more relevant than ever. Having both music videos (based on your recorded tracks) and live performance videos are important. A lot of concert buyers are now looking for live performance videos to book dates. Make sure that you have links to these from your site. A lot of contests, funding programs and showcase festivals are requiring live performance videos in their applications.

Link to your YouTube or Vimeo channel. There is no need to house content on your site, however try and embed the player into your site instead of sending visitors to the host site. Most video hosting sites provide the code to embed their players. If you can keep the viewer on your site, that is the best-case scenario. Internet users can be easily distracted by pretty lights, kittens and other things…

e. **Mailing list sign up.** This should be placed on the top right corner of the homepage where you can't miss it. Request email, social media connections and city of residence from your fans. At a minimum, get their email. Mailing lists are incredibly valuable to your sustained career. Owning your own database is critical. The ability to communicate directly with your fans is a tool that cannot be overstated.

Consider using a service like Mailchimp to manage your fan emails and newsletter. The fan information can be set up to go automatically to the Mailchimp mailing list database (make sure that you export your fan data periodically). Then, you can simply send newsletters from there. Mailchimp allows you to set up newsletter templates so that you can simply add the latest news and send to everyone in the database. Remember to work smarter, not harder!

f. **Social media links and feeds** (links on home page using social media logos and home page social media feeds). Have links to all your social media such as Twitter, Facebook, Instagram, Soundcloud, and Bandcamp. In addition, having the actual feeds from Twitter, Facebook and other social media running on your web site is an easy way to ensure that there is a constant flow of news on your site. People who visit your site may be intrigued by the dialogue and want to participate. Consider adding a RSS (Rich Site Summary) link to ensure that your fans get constant updates from your site.

g. **Blog.** More and more artists have blogs these days. A blog is a periodic artist web posting that can literally be about anything. Most often, it is a running dialogue as to the artist's progress. Artists have a lot to say and creating a blog is a way to engage your fans in a deeper dialogue than Facebook and Twitter will allow. Tumblr is a popular blog hosting site that you can use to host your blog. The Mother Mother Blog is a fantastic example of a successful band blog. The Lefsetz Letter is a great example of a music industry blog. You may want to consider subscribing.

h. **News.** (home page posting). Part of your publicity plan will be sending out press releases. The news section of your site should hit on the high points of your activities. Tour launch, album release, award nominations and wins and other significant news can be added here. Having a news section on your home page is a great way to ensure that you are always keeping your site up to date.

i. **Concert listings**. Letting your fans know well in advance as to where you are playing is going to help make sure that ticket sales stay high. With today's high concert ticket prices, people are far more picky as to what shows they see. The more lead time that you give them, the better the chance that they may choose your show over others.

j. **Contact.** Make it easy to get ahold of you and your reps. This area is where you put all of your team contacts. At first this will be your contact only, but over time you can add your manager, agent, label, publisher, publicist, and fan club contacts.

k. **Store.** Last, but certainly not least, having a store is essential. If you have released online, then link to various online stores, especially iTunes. Make sure that you have CDs and merch available online. The impulse buyer at your concert may have regretted not standing in line to buy your CD and T-shirt. Make it easy for them and fill the orders right away. I have found that Paypal is the easiest and most used e-commerce solution to manage the financial transactions from an online store.

Update Constantly. Update your online content very frequently; at least weekly. An easy way to do this is to integrate your social media feeds with your website. If your Twitter feed is on the home page, then people can see that you are active and will continue to come back. Posting your news on a regular basis on the home page of your site is also a great way to keep the website fresh. Consider holding back content such as videos so that you have something to add over a longer period of time. Some bands have been launching all of their album videos in quick succession. You may want to consider being patient and allowing yourself some time and space to keep things interesting for your fans.

Social Media and the 80/20 rule. Credit has to be given where credit is due. Blogger Brian Thompson told me about the 80/20 rule. People do not participate in social media to be sold to, however I have found that most artists spend 90% of their time pushing gigs and releases down everyone's throats. It is noise and for the most part it is ignored. Successful artists are the ones who engage their fans online. People want to have a dialogue, to be part of something. That is what Facebook and Twitter are truly about. So, as an artist you need to figure out your own way to engage your fans 80% of the time. If you can do that, you can earn the right to sell to these fans 20% of the time. It is simple and it works. For example, don't say, "Buy tickets to our gig this Friday here". Say, "We have some new music and want your opinion. Check out the demos here. What do you think?" Engage in a discussion with the fans before telling them about your show. Be genuinely interested in their stories. Put a question at the end of a blog or status update. This creates an invitation to discuss. I tried this for the first time about a year ago and I haven't looked back. It is highly effective.

Content is King on Youtube. Have amazing online content. People are drawn to creativity. If you produce something stellar, people will hear about it and want to see it. Word-of-mouth online can explode virally. For example, in 2012 some film students in Montreal were challenged by their professor to create a viral video. They produced a CGI clip of an eagle snatching a child at a park called Golden Eagle Snatches Kid Within hours this became an international sensation and they had millions of views. The video has had over 40 million views. While it was a hoax, it does illustrate the power of creating something compelling and provoking.

A few years ago, an artist named Jeremy Fisher created an animated video of his song "Cigarette". This was done on his iMac with a micro-budget. It featured an animated cigarette going around his apartment. It was creative, compelling and got him noticed in a big way. He received over 2 million views and a deal offer from a New York based music company.

Success online is not about spending the most money, it is about being the most creative. Setting up a YouTube account to monetize your views is a good idea. You have to set up an account with Google AdSense. Google now owns YouTube and pays on views that have an authorized ad preceding the video. The only problem is that, in round terms, the payment is about $1500 for 1 million views. But remember that this is a business of pennies and you want to make sure that you capitalize if one of your videos takes off. Gangnam Style is now at nearly 2 billion YouTube views. Do the math. Need I say more?

One great way to get better use from your YouTube views is to add annotations to your videos directing people to your website or where they can buy your music. Go to your video manager page. On each video, there is an edit pull-down. Under that is the annotation option. You can add short messages to videos for your viewers. This is a great tool to push interested fans to your store.

Facebook

Whether we like it or not, Facebook has become a big part of our every day lives. For now, it is the place to be, the place to go, the place to communicate. As an artist, you need to be on Facebook.

Facebook is set up primarily as a communication tool between friends. Your "Timeline" or "Profile" is the main place to interact personally with your friends. The Profile is not meant for commercial activations. Facebook created Pages that can be set up under your profile for more commercial activities. That is where you can set up a Band Page. The band page on Facebook allows you to post events and status updates to your fans. Band Pages build fans with "likes".

Facebook Pages

Facebook has monetized the Pages sections of their site. This means that in order for you to reach the fans who have "liked" your Band Page you need to pay "boost" your updates. In addition, you can choose to advertise events, status updates or create your own ads on the platform. The "organic reach" (reach to your fans without paying) is now very low; perhaps 10% of your fans will get a post without payment. As an artist, you will have to decide whether Facebook ads are effective for you. You may want to talk to a publicist who specializes in social media to come up with an impactful plan to maximize your social media impact.

Facebook allows you to post events on your Band Page. Certainly do this. Post your gigs and tours as Facebook events. Understand, however, that for the most part Event postings have become noise to most people. It is good to have your events posted, but if you stop there, then you are truly missing the real benefit of Facebook.

Facebook Profile or Timeline

For the time being, your Profile page will continue to get "organic reach", but how far your reach will get is now based on an algorithm that calculates the friend engagement that you have. The most important thing to remember about using Facebook is that it is really about building a community around you. Build your friends one at a time. Don't be lazy. When someone asks to be a friend, check out their Facebook page before approving them. Find something that you have in common with this new friend. After you accept them, write a short message thanking them for the friend request. Say something in the message that shows that you took the time to look at their page. If you genuinely make your friends feel important then they will support you when you need it. It may come to the point where you have too many friends to be able to do this for every one. When you get to that point, check out as many new friends as you can. Never stop making personal connections with your fans. That is the essence of social media: one-on-one contact.

Facebook is about building a community around you. Your Facebook friends want to hear what you have to say. More importantly they want to interact with you. That means creating a dialogue and allowing them to participate. When you update your status, always invite a response. Get in the habit of ending each status update with an invitation to talk about the issue that you are bringing up. Remember the 80/20 rule. Resist the temptation to sell all the time. Being excited about your new release or your tour is great, but you need to figure out a way to bring your "friends" into your excitement without overtly selling to them. For example, if you are going to play in Calgary don't just announce the date. Say something like, "We are on the road now and rolling into Calgary tomorrow. Where can we get the best ribs in town?"

Facebook last thoughts

Notwithstanding the above thoughts, there are some direct selling opportunities presented by Facebook. Facebook has made it easy and relatively inexpensive to target advertising to specific Facebook users. You can drill down quite deeply into your target demographic. While some artists that I have worked with have not had a huge return on investment through Facebook also provides very detailed analytics. You can use this to help promote crowd source funding campaigns, releases, tours and other band announcements.

Twitter

This microblogging site allows only 140 character messages to be sent out into the ether. While a good percentage of the content is useless babble, there is a lot of very useful communication. There is certainly a Twitter language that you need to be aware of. Your tweets can be seen by anyone, but your "followers" get fed your tweets because they have opted into receiving them. Each registered user has an address designated with an "@". For example, my Twitter handle is @bobdeith. If you tweet a message that involves a person or a company in some way, then you should include their handle in your tweet. They will receive your message whether or not they are a follower. Often, if they like the message they will re-tweet it to their followers. This is a fantastic way to get your messages out and add new followers.

The other big Twitter language issue is the hashtag. Messages with hashtags will be picked up by the system and ranked according to the number of people using that hashtag. For example, #thepeakpp is used during the Peak Performance Project. All of the artists are encouraged to use this hashtag in their tweets. At times, #thepeakpp has "trended" in Canada when there is a huge amount of activity. A hashtag will trend when it is recognized as the top ranked hashtag in the area, whether that is within a city, a province, a country or in the world.

While there are only 140 characters allowed, Twitter allows you to link to URL's and rich media links. This is a great way to get the word out about tour listings on your site or a new video on YouTube.

One very valuable tool is the Twitter search engine. You can search for similar artists and then follow their followers. Most people will follow back once someone follows them. This is a great way to build up a Twitter following with people who will probably be interested in your music.

Another great tool is Clicktotweet. This site allows you make it easy for your followers to tweet for you.

LinkedIn (industry)

The value of LinkedIn for artists is that this is where the music business connects. While LinkedIn was initially set up primarily for job postings and referrals, recently it has grown into a massive business forum. There are some incredible resources and discussion groups in LinkedIn. Many of the leaders in the music industry have a presence on this platform. You should consider participating in the discussions. Remember not to sell your music right away. Imagine if you went to a meeting with a music publisher and the first thing out of your mouth was "check out my demo." Get to know the players first and then slide in your music later.

Flickr, Instagram and Snapchat (pictures)

Every smartphone has a camera now. This means that there are infinite possibilities to document your exploits. Flickr and Instagram are great sites to host your pictures on. It is easy to upload pictures to both platforms from your iPhone or computer. Once on Flickr or Instagram, it is easy to link your pictures to your fans.

There is no question that Snapchat is the most used picture app by tweens and teens today. If your demographic aims at this group, then you should seriously consider trying to develop a strategy around Snapchat.

Tumblr (blog hosting).

One great way to engage your fans is to Blog. This doesn't have to be just written blogs. Video blogging has become extremely popular. Video blogging allows for a really intimate insight into your thoughts and life. Remember though, only you can decide how much of yourself that you want to give away. Written blogs are also very useful in engaging your fan base. While perhaps a little less intimate than video blogs, the written blog can be highly creative outlet for you as well. I have read some amazingly thought provoking blogs from artists over the years.

Hootsuite. With all of the social media out there, you may want to use an aggregated service like Hootsuite to manage your social media. Hootsuite allows you to send to multiple social media posts simultaneously on a schedule you decide. This service also allows you to monitor all of the social media dialogues from one place. One tip, be careful in regard to different social media "language". For example, Twitter page references (@) on Facebook has the tendency to annoy some Facebook users if they show up in your

Facebook posts.

Email. Many online gurus say that email as a form of communication is dying. Most people are using social media to communicate and that is growing. While this may be true to a certain extent, I still find that email is my principal way of direct messaging to clients, fans and the industry. As mentioned above, services like Mailchimp use email in a very effective way. Mailchimp also integrates Facebook and Twitter into your newsletter messaging. There is a danger though. Bulk emails can end up being picked up as spam at the other end.

Another observation is that sending out emails that are not personalized to the receiver have far less impact than those that are personalized. It is far more time consuming, but exponentially more effective, to send targeted and personalized emails. If you can send out emails with even one line showing that you are actually sending a one-on-one email, then there is a much better chance of the email being opened, read and responded to. This is where getting to know your fans as individuals can really pay off. Your superfans are fans who love to talk about you, show up at every gig and eat up everything that you send out. They will have the most word-of-mouth impact and should be your priority. On the other hand, they are also the ones that are "this close" to a restraining order. There is a fine line between superfan and stalker.

Even though it takes time, consider actually checking out each fan's Facebook profile to see what their interests are. If you have something in common, you can use that to connect with them directly. For example:

Subject line: Hey Jim! The Walking Dead are coming to Halifax June 16, 20XX [personalized headline to get their interest]

Dear Jim, [addressed directly to the fan]

I see that we are both Radiohead fans. That band had a major influence on our music. [Information that you found on Jim's Facebook page for a personalized message]

Anyway, guess what? We are coming to your town in a few weeks and hope that you will come down. You can pick up tickets at…. [cut and paste message]

Check out a video of our live show [hyperlink to YouTube]

All the best,

Fred Zombie
The Walking Dead

Email "subject lines" are critical. I often get 3-400 emails a day and I know of people in the industry who get many more than that. For the most part, people screen their emails by first seeing who the email is from and second by looking at the subject line. The best-case scenario is that the receiver can get the main message from the subject line. Consider it like the headline of a newspaper article. The subject line should capture the attention of the reader. However, do not make your subject lines too generic or they risk being flagged as spam.

As far as communicating with anyone via email, whether to a fan or industry, never, ever send attachments that are not requested or expected. Music industry professionals prefer to receive an email with a hyperlinked connection to a download page. Use a service like Dropbox or Box over something like Hightail (formerly YouSendIt), because emails get archived and may be checked months after they are sent. If the download link expires with time, like Hightail, then the person receiving the email may not be able to get the content that they want. Do not ever expect anyone in the industry to ask you for another link. Normally, they will just move on as they have too little time.

Some other communication tips:

a. **Short and sweet.** No one has time for long essays. Get to the point.
b. **Proof read.** Before you hit send always read through your messages one last time. Auto-correct can do some funny things to emails. Check out Damn You Auto Correct to see what I mean. You may only have one chance to make a lasting impression, so make sure that you take the time to get it right.
c. **Cc's can be dangerous**, especially if you are in the middle of an email chain. I have certainly cc'ed a few email chains that should not have gone to one of the receivers. Always be careful with what you are sending or you risk burning bridges, or having to buy a bottle or wine for one of your sponsors (just saying).
d. **There is a time to email and there is a time to pick up the phone.** We are all capable of getting too emotional with email. We will say things with email that we might not say over the phone or face-to-face. If you are getting to that point with an email exchange, pick up the phone. There is no subtlety to an email. The recipient of an email cannot read your tone or your body language. Emails can be misconstrued very easily. So, if things get heated, make the phone call or set up a personal meeting before things get out of hand.

Online tools and social media are there to help you network and communicate. The more your blast out information without taking the time to dialogue, the more your messaging simply becomes noise. Always remember that people do not go online to be sold to. They go online for information, entertainment, dialogue, and interaction with their peers. Show that you care for your fans by getting to know them and they will be fans for life.

For further insight into social media and how this phenomenon has changed so much in the way that we work and live I suggest reading Erik Qualman's books "Socialnomics" and "Digital Leader" Erik Qualman. His basic concept that you need to listen before you sell is of fundamental importance to success online.

Chapter 8 Success with the Media

Grant Lawrence, a media personality with CBC Radio 3, lectures on Making Friends with the Media. One of the key messages from his talk is that the media can be an ally in the development of an artist's career. Certainly, the press can be brutal to famous artists, but Madonna taught us all that there is really no such thing as bad press. In fact, sometimes it seems that some pop artists are addicted to press – good or bad.

Grant put me on to an amazing example of what not to do in an interview. Watch the interview with Sigur Ros on NPR's Bryant Park Project and then note all of the things that went wrong. The end of this chapter I present some ideas as to what I think makes this one of the worst interviews ever.

Radio, print, television, online and all other media crave content. They need stories to get eyeballs in order to sell advertising. Your job is to give them a story. That is the basic problem with most bios and press releases – they tend to be generic and give the press nothing to work with. For example, an artist is doing a CD release so they send a press release out to all the media sources. Unfortunately, these same media sources receive hundreds of other press releases and without a compelling story to go with, it might merely become background noise. Now, if that same artist put some thought into how they could interest the press, then the CD release might have been part of a bigger story – the artist was banned from metro Toronto because their name was considered offensive, or the artist was unfortunately detained by Chinese police for having bullet casings in one of their bags, or the artist raised $20,000 for a local charity, or the album was the result of winning a big radio contest. All of these examples are true stories. Do you know who they are? If so, then the story caught your attention through the media.

Building Relationships. The next big lesson about dealing with the media is that you need to build a relationship. If you are starting locally, then you can easily find out who the local music writers are. Get to know them. Keep them in the loop. Be pleasantly persistent but never aggressive, annoying or in people's faces. A former music director of a Vancouver radio station told me that Nickelback used to bring Slurpees into the station every Friday for the staff. This allowed the band to get to know and make contacts. When their albums came out, people wanted to support them. In fact, Chad used this same strategy in early radio tracking by calling the music directors personally. He would talk about everything other than the release before mentioning the actual reason for the call. He got to know the people that could impact his career and after some time they wanted to help him and his band.

Commercial Radio. A discussion of the media would not be complete without discussing the impact of traditional commercial radio on an artist's career. Unfortunately, commercial radio is a very narrow pipeline in terms of the type of music that is played. Only a small percentage of recordings produced are ever played on commercial radio. The other problem lies in the fact that commercial radio has been consolidating for years now. This means that playlists are often controlled nationally by one music director. Consider that getting onto commercial radio means producing songs that fit into specific formats: Country, CHR, Rock, Hot AC, AC and AAA. Within these genres, there are specific sub-genres that will be played and others that will not. Also, keep in mind that what is a "hit" can change over time as trends evolve. In the last few years (2010-2013), there has been a movement towards Alternative Rock with folk and blues roots, with bands like The Black Keys, Fun and Mumford & Sons. The 80's saw hair rock and new wave, the 90's saw rock, alternative and grunge, 2000's were dominated by hip hop, pop punk and alt rock. The point is that times change and with it commercial radio. As mentioned before, my advice to you in this regard is never chase a trend. By the time you have released something in that trend, the trend has changed. Be true to what you do and do it well. If you are after commercial radio, however, make sure that what you are producing fits the formats that are out there.

Radio Trackers. You may want to consider hiring a radio tracker to help you get commercial radio play. Radio trackers are like publicists who specialize in getting songs on the radio. As with all of your marketing money, be careful with hiring a radio tracker. You may find that you get more action from doing it yourself. If you do so, you may want to consider using the DMDS service to get your song out to commercial radio and then track the progress yourself. If you need help with the radio servicing process, I would recommend RDR Music Group. Joe Wood and his team make it easy to get your music out to commercial radio. If you do not have a tracker, then you will need to register your song with BDS in order for it to be properly tracked and will get on the charts (BDS Radio Registration). A radio tracker would do this registration for you.

If you decide to go with a radio tracker, there are some advantages to doing so. A good radio tracker already has the relationships with radio and can often help get you charting. There are a few radio trackers like Tandemtracks Promotion or Frontside Group who will give you an honest opinion as to your chances to get played. If they take your money, they will work hard for you. There are also radio trackers out there who will gladly take your money and put you in with the other five or six artists that they are tracking (two of which they have publishing interests in). So, do your homework, ask other artists and treat your limited marketing dollars like treasure.

If you are not really a commercial radio artist, that is fine. Just do not have unrealistic expectations about getting on the radio. Having said that, it is interesting how things can happen. My group Mythos is an ambient instrumental duo. We do not generally use lyrics, but use vocals as an instrument. We had zero expectations of commercial radio. Then, Enigma, Delerium and Robert Miles happened in the mid-1990s. We managed to get a commercial radio hit because a very, very small window opened for us. So, never say never!

Non-commercial radio. The reality is that most of the music produced is not suitable for traditional commercial radio. So where can you go? Campus, Community, Co-Op, internet, satellite, digital and other non-traditional commercial or non-commercial radio are all out there for you. The problem is that listenership is not at the level that will normally generate record sales. SOCAN public performance royalty checks for such play are very low. It is still great for general marketing and promotion, so go after everything that you can. These stations normally want to receive entire albums as opposed to "singles".

CBC RADIO. CBC is a fantastic resource for those artists who are not appropriate for commercial radio. CBC Radio 1, CBC Radio 2, CBC Radio 3 (CBC Radio 3 is an online service) all share the same song pool. A great thing about CBC radio play is that each play is tracked and generates public performance royalties. CBC is incredibly supportive to independent music in Canada. Cultivating a relationship with CBC and its various programs could be of immense help to your career.

Publicists. What about using a publicist to get noticed by the media? Publicists can be a great help as they already have the relationships with the people that you need to reach in the media. The trick is to use a publicist when you actually need one. So when do you need a publicist? When you have a story to tell. When you need help getting a really great hook out there. How about some examples of when and when not to hire a publicist:

a. We are having a CD release party! NO, CD's are becoming an anachronism. In all seriousness, there is a CD release every few hours and there is nothing special about that.

b. We are releasing a single with an accompanying video with a surprise cameo from Ellen DeGeneres. Hell ya. How did that happen? When can we get you on CBC to talk about that?

c. We are touring Ontario. NO, do you know how many bands are touring in Ontario? What is particularly special about that? If there is a hook, then maybe, but ask yourself why the media would care.

d. We twisted Ralph James' arm at the Agency Group and he is putting the band on tour with Nickelback. YES, that is a story. Hire a publicist.

e. We are an indie Canadian band from Saskatchewan and we have been shortlisted on a contest to get on the front of Rolling Stone magazine. YES, spin that.

By the way, all of the above examples resulting in a YES are actual examples of bands. Two of them are pretty easy to guess, one is a bit more challenging, but you can find it on YouTube if you search carefully. If you are curious, see the answers at the end of this chapter.

Some great Canadian publicists who have helped me, my organizations and my clients:

Killbeat Music, Fritz Media, Strut Entertainment, Hype Music, Modmay Promotions.

Public Speaking

"According to most studies, people's number one fear is public speaking. Number two is death. Death is number two! Now, this means to the average person, if you have to go to a funeral, you're better off in the casket than doing the eulogy." (Jerry Seinfeld).

I have never had any formal media training, but I have certainly had lots of great coaching. In particular, Tamara Stanners from 102.7 The PEAK has been an amazing mentor for me. Tamara loves everyone and everything, so it was quite eye opening when she came up to me after one Peak Performance Project speech and told me that I really sucked. Public speaking and dealing with the media are both very inter-related. Tamara's best advice to me was to be *interesting and engaging, not informational and boring.* She thought that I sounded like a lawyer and that she saw people's eyes glaze over. I really try now to make sure that my presentations are interesting and more entertaining. If I can add some humour, that is also good, especially when dealing with a dry topic.

This same advice can definitely apply to the media. Being on television or on the radio, playing the cool artist, answering evasively and with one-word answers can make you look like an ass. I am not saying that you should suddenly transform into Carrot Top and be a clown, but balance your self-image with a recognition that the audience is hungry to get to know you and your art. Only you can decide how much of yourself you are willing to give up, but in the end making that personal connection with your listeners is what is going to make them real fans. That same principal applies to social media. You need to give to get, just decide how much you are comfortable sharing.

Preparation is key.

"It usually takes more than three weeks to prepare a good impromptu speech." *Mark Twain.* One interesting phenomenon is when some artists, who night after night put themselves out there as vocalists or musicians, clam up when dealing with the media. Artists who are willing to stage dive and whip a crowd into a frenzy suddenly become shy when faced with an interview or media appearance. I think the answer to this is preparation. You are in your comfort zone as a recording or live performance artist. It is what you know and understand. Talking on radio or television, or having to answer tough interview questions for newspapers and magazines can be daunting. If you follow these simple rules, you might become more comfortable and effective in dealing with the press:

    a. Always know what your message is in advance. What are you trying to get across to the media? Tour dates, music recording release, video release? Politicians know this one well. "Does anyone have any questions for my answers?" (Henry Kissinger).

    b. Remember that you can always steer the interview to where you want it to go. You will learn this over time and practice, but good interviewees can seamlessly transition a discussion into the direction that they want. This also plays into the first rule.

c. Never be ashamed of who you are and where you are from. I have heard from many, many media people that they really want to know where you actually came from. It is OK that you are from a small town in Alberta or Newfoundland. In fact, that is what makes your story unique.

d. Adjust your delivery to the media that you are presenting to. If you are on radio, remember that no one can see you. You have to verbalize everything. If you are on TV remember that they can see you and your non-verbal responses. Look confident and engaged.

e. Don't take the entire band on every media date. Send the appropriate one or two members for the interview.

f. Be on time. Media work to deadlines and if you are not there when you are supposed to be, you will not only miss your interview, you may burn a bridge. Also, you never want to feel rushed. Give yourself time to prepare ahead of the interview.

OK, Sigur Ros. Great band from Iceland, but probably gave the worse band interview I have ever seen. What did they do wrong? (a) Nodding answers on the radio, (b) big silences, (c) one word answers, (d) looking at each other instead of answering the question, (e) not taking control of the interview, (f) too many members on the air – should have been one or two max, (g) gave stupid answers to the questions asked, (h) were not prepared for the interview and (i) did not have a clear message for the interview. There is more, but you can see how important it is to be prepared for the media. Over 200,000 people have seen this bad interview. So what do you think that does for the band's career?

Publicity answers:

a. N/A
b. Behind Sapphire
c. N/A
d. State of Shock
e. The Sheepdogs

Chapter 9 Treat your music career as a business

If you treat your career as a great excuse to party, then you will probably be going through the other 12-step program, know what I am saying?

Artists often shy away from the idea of treating their career like a business. It seems contrary to the creative process to think like a "suit". The reality of today's music business is that you cannot afford to wait around for someone to rescue you. Many artists ask me how they can get a manager, but I always say that you will not get a manager until you have something to manage. Managers get paid as a percentage of your gross revenues. 20% of $0 is $0.

Build it and they will come. In order to succeed in this new music business paradigm, you need to become a savvy business person. Once you have achieved a certain level of success, the team members will naturally be attracted to you. You create your own luck by building the parts of your career that result in success. For example, if you have built your live guarantee up to $1000 per night, an agent might get interested as picking up the phone will make him $100. If you tour Canada three or four times and get a buzz going in a few cities, a manager may take notice. If you are able to sell 20,000 singles on iTunes, A&R (the people who look for talent to sign) at a label may perk up their ears. If you get radio play and a few great film and TV placements, a music publisher may see the value in partnering with you.

Join your local Music Industry Association. Do yourself a big favour: join your provincial music industry association. Contacts for all the "MIAs" can be found on the CCMIA website. If you are in Ontario, the CIMA recently created a provincial music industry association called Music Ontario .The MIAs are non-profit societies committed to the development of artists and the music industry in their provinces or territories. This includes export marketing, networking, music business education workshops, funding, discount programs, directories and many other services. The MIAs also work together to advocate for artist and music industry rights in Canada. The CCMIA has developed the tourhub.ca web and mobile tool by linking all of the MIA venue databases. This app helps artists and artist reps book tours. It is a free service open to all Canadians. The MIAs have also formed alliances with other organizations such as the Western Canadian Music Alliance. This alliance produces BreakOut West and the Western Canadian Music Awards. Attending this conference, festival and award show is a great way to build your contacts and network in the industry.

If you are a band, have a band agreement. Another big part of building your success is taking care of your own house. That means you need to have all of the business registrations and contracts in place. In my experience, a band is, by definition, a dysfunctional family. Having a "pre-nuptial" agreement of sorts is a really good idea. You hope that you will never break up, but you do not have statistics on your side, just like marriages.

As a group, you need to deal with all the basic issues set out in the Part 2 Chapter 8 Band Agreements in order to ensure the ability to make deals when the time comes. What happens when a big brewery wants to use your song and the old bass player with a small songwriting credit is out of the country and cannot sign off? What happens if the drummer leaves the band and will not release her interest in the band name? What happens if the trailer with all your gear is stolen and you did not bother to think about insurance? These are all based on true stories and cases that I have had personal experience with as a lawyer. It can easily happen to you.

The same goes for agreements with producers, side performers, tour managers and everyone else that you do business with. Take care of the business side or you will end up frustrated when opportunities pass you by.

Funding

FACTOR and RADIO STARMAKER. In Canada, we are very fortunate to have funding for the arts, musicians and music companies. FACTOR, The Foundation to Assist Canadian Talent On Recordings, grants funding of about $15 million per year. These funds go to everything from demo recording to album recording, marketing and promotion, tour support, video production, and funding of industry associations.

The first thing you will need to do is register a "User" profile on the Factor site. This is simply to allow Factor to recognize you when you login to their system. Then, you will need to register an "Artist" profile. Factor has determined a 1-3 rating system for artists based on various criteria for recent success. This "Artist" profile should be updated whenever something significant happens and should be accounted for. Factor reassesses artist profiles periodically to see if an artist has increased their rating. For most artists, they will be assessed a "1" rating. A "1" rating means that applications for funding must go through the jury process. Once an artist has reached a certain track record, their rating in the system will go up to 2 or 3. Once an artist reaches a 3 rating, they will be able to apply for funding through the Comprehensive Artist Program without having to go through a jury process.

Once an artist has received a rating, then the artist will know which programs the artist is eligible for. When an artist wants to apply, then the artist can submit an "Application". The program applications include Demo, Sound Recording, Live Performance, Radio Marketing, Songwriter Workshop and others.

One of the great moves that Factor has made is authorizing a pre-approved marketing component of the sound recording program. If an artist is successful in receiving Sound Recording funding (whether juried on non-juried), Factor will help fund the promotion of that recording. The marketing can include video production, tour support, web design, Facebook advertising and a wide range of marketing and promotion activities.

A similar path of ratings exists with Factor for labels. Labels are rated on success on a 1-5 rating basis. This will determine whether a label must apply through the juries sound recording process or whether they can get funding through the Comprehensive Label Program.

Radio Starmaker also has millions of dollars per year to put into more established artists careers. If you have reached a significant level of achievement in your genre, researching the eligibility criteria for application to the Starmaker programs would be prudent. In fact, looking at Factor and Radio Starmaker eligibility criteria can act as great goals for an Artist.

Grant Writing.

Accessing these loans and grants is the topic of a separate book. My general advice is to treat your applications with the same care and quality as you would when sending out your materials to senior people in the industry. Make sure that EVERY part of your application is first rate. In fact, you can pull from many of the chapters in this book to help you prepare for successful applications. Your promotional materials, recordings and marketing plan are going to be essential in this process. If you applying through a jury process, do not give them any excuse to turn you down. You are only as strong as your weakest link – bad picture, pitchy vocals, typos, incomplete marketing plan – these are all examples of reasons to reject your application. Be specific and realistic in your applications and you will do well. As far as grant writers, use them but be careful. If they do not create materials that are unique to you, especially the marketing plan, then they are not doing their job. Use of a generic template marketing plan provided by a grant writer is not helpful.

Music Industry Association funding.

Each province has its own music industry association that administers varying amounts of provincial artist development funding. Check out your local provincial MIA on the CCMIA website. Another great source of funding is the Canada Council for the Arts, but please keep in mind that the genres that can access these funds are primarily limited to classical, jazz, folk, world, experimental electronic and other "more artistic than commercial" types of music.

There are two main sources of funding programs for artists. One is Canadian Content Development funding ("CCD") from radio broadcasters and the other is government funding (from all levels of government). CCD funding helps to fund FACTOR, Radio Starmaker and a myriad of other programs nationally. CCD funding is triggered whenever there is a new radio license or sale of a license. When broadcasters are bidding for a new license, 7 year CCD funding can become a big part of their proposal to the CRTC. One case in point is the Peak Performance Project ("PPP") that Music BC administers for Jim Pattison Broadcasting.

Peak Performance Project. In BC (2009-2015) and Alberta (2014-2020), the PEAK radio stations are committed to over $10 million in artist development funding. At the beginning of the program in BC, Music BC worked closely with Jim Pattison Broadcasting to develop a program that would be as impactful as possible for the music community. The PPP is designed to integrate education, significant funding, showcasing, marketing and promotion as well as radio play from commercial radio. The program takes 20 artists per year and showcases them together. The artists go through an intensive one-week bootcamp (in Rockridge Canyon, Princeton, BC), perform in some adjudicated showcases, and participate in various career enhancing challenges. Finally the top 3 perform at a major venue and share $225,000 in artist development funding. The purpose of the program is to help artists get to the next level in their career path and to give them the tools to sustain a career in music. Winners have included We Are The City, Said The Whale, Kyprios, Current Swell, The Boom Booms, The Matinee, Jordan Klassen, Dominique Fricot, Bend Sinister and others. One winner, Dear Rouge, truly embraced the process and showed everyone what can happen if you take charge of your career. Dear Rouge formed only months before the program and only squeaked into the Top 20. There were other artists much farther ahead in terms of touring and fan base. However, from the moment they entered the program, they took everything that we gave them and put 100% in every category from songwriting, to fundraising for their charity ($17,500), to getting local press (front page of the Vancouver Province), to creating an amazing viral video. Their live show was one of the best and their online voting was very high. That is how they won $102,700.00. They earned their way into it. That same kind of attitude put into every day artist development can lead any talented artist to achieving great success.

Investment

Crowdsource funding online. Indiegogo.com , Kickstarter.com and Pledgemusic are two examples of sites where artists have been able to raise investment funding for their various projects. There are many other crowdsourcing sites as well. This practice has become very popular with artists and the public. These types of services have given the public an outlet to get directly involved in developing artist careers. There are stories of indie bands raising tens of thousands of dollars this way. Bands have found all sorts of innovative ways to get investors interested from giving credits on albums, to actually performing on tracks, to exclusive live access, to personal performances and many other offers that in most cases are easy for the artist, but priceless for the investor. Don't undervalue the sizzle of being a band or an artist in the music biz. Many investors have always wanted to do what you are doing and desire to live vicariously through you. This is a good thing.

Private investment is quite common as well. You need to decide whether you want to give an investor a share of your future revenues or whether you would simply like to pay them back with interest.

Investment Versus Loan:

Normally an investment means that you only pay the investor once you are profitable. If the project fails under an investment, then the investor often simply loses all their money.

With a loan, the investor is acting as a bank and normally expects to be paid back with interest. The level of investment risk determines how much of a slice of your revenue pie that investor will get.

When CD sales were still viable in stores, investors would get a return from sales but as retail has collapsed, smart investors are now insisting on sharing in live performance, publishing and merch as well as recording sales revenue.

Music Lawyers.

It is very important to have a lawyer involved in any investment situation as there are a number of ways to structure deals. Find a music lawyer in your area. You should engage a lawyer any time that you get a significant deal offer. As far as live shows, you may have to deal with that yourself until you have an agent. Any kind of deal such as your band agreement, a producer agreement, licensing agreement, artist agreement, publishing agreement (of any type), get a music lawyer (and this does not mean your uncle Joe the real estate lawyer). Please feel free to contact me for legal advice. My contact information is available in the appendices to this book.

Chapter 10 Planning for success

"I feel that luck is preparation meeting opportunity" (Oprah Winfrey - net worth $2.7 BILLION).

I am a huge believer that in the music business you make your own luck. Many artists get frustrated that nothing is happening in their careers,but are unwilling to put in the hard work and persistence that is required for success. Being in the right place at the right time and gaining opportunities is more often a product of hard work than it is coincidence. Sure, there are always stories of the "get rich quick" artists, but usually if you dig even slightly below the surface, you will see a driven and ambitious artist focused on success.

There are different kinds of plans that artists can make. In fact, every part of the artist's career can be planned. Goal setting is very helpful in order to focus your energy in the right direction. However, always remember that "those who plan do better than those who do not plan even though they rarely stick to their plan" (Winston Churchill). In other words, make a plan, but don't be so married to it that you cannot adapt to changes in that plan. When I talk about planning, I am not talking about setting rigid steps that end up hampering your success. There is still the very great need to "just do it". You are an entrepreneur and must be constantly thinking outside the box, especially in the volatile and constantly shifting digital world that we live in.

"A business has to be involving, it has to be fun, and it has to exercise your creative instincts." (Richard Branson - founder of Virgin). Most musicians that I know do not apply their creative energy to planning and marketing. In fact, the same creativity that is used in songwriting and performing can and should be harnessed in the designing of your business and marketing plans. It is ironic to me that some of the most creative people that I know have the most unimaginative plans. Have some fun with it. Try and figure out an innovative ways to promote yourself. Use your talents. I have had the pleasure of working with Hilary Grist, a singer-songwriter. Hilary is also a very talented visual artist. She has been able to integrate her ability to draw into her marketing in many ways – website design, animated videos, interesting merch.

In Rymes with Orange, a lot of our success was due to creative marketing. Even the choice of the band name was part of this thinking. We had our own custom made wrapping paper for our demos, we would send boxes of oranges to industry reps, and we created merch that played on our name (Rymes with !@#$% all).

With Mythos, our artwork became a very important part of our marketing. Matching the sound with compelling images (artist Gil Bruvel) really helped connect us with the fans. These images can be seen at Mythos Website. Use that non-linear brain that you already have to create amazing marketing plans.

Don't rush releases. As a recording artist and musician, you will want to share your music with everyone as soon as it is created. I get that. You are excited and proud, and you feel that this time you have made something that will resonate around the world. RESIST THESE FEELINGS. We are our own worst enemies when it comes to our own music business issues.

A typical first indie artist release example is as follows:

      a. album is finished and immediately released on Tunecore to the entire world,
      b. three months later a song is released to radio,
      c. two months after that the band gets a video up on YouTube,
      d. then the band starts booking a local tour…..and on and on.

Can you see the problem? There is no strategy to this release and by the time the band actually gets on the road the album is already old.

Planning allows you to think about your strategy (general plan of action leading to complicated goals) and tactics (how you are going to specifically achieve these goals). Let's look at the above release. What is the strategy behind recording a full-length album? Are albums still relevant in today's market? Perhaps. But, would it be better to have released an EP? A single? Why did this band rush out the album without first having touring, radio, publicity, video and other plans in place? Was this course of action "proactive" or "reactive"? This line of questioning could go on for hours. The long and the short of it is that there has to be a reason why you are taking action and there has to be a plan to implement those actions. Everything you do should be connected and impactful.

So, what kind of plans should you consider?

A business plan lays out your overall business strategy for success and includes forecasts of revenues and how you are going to achieve them. These are really useful in securing investors and convincing your parents that you actually have a "real job".

A marketing plan can form part of a business plan or be a stand-alone document. Most funding applications require a Marketing Plan. The Marketing Plan sets out how you intend to market what you are planning to do, whether that is a recording release, tour and/or radio release.

Part 2 to this book gives you an annotated outline of a Marketing Plan for a sound recording release and the outline of a Business Plan. Plans should never be generic. To be effective, they should be realistic, specific and tailored to your particular needs.

If you hire a consultant to help with planning, make sure you are not being sold a "template". Make your consultants earn their money by drafting a plan that make sense to you and is particular to your situation.

When you release a track, an EP or an album, there are a number of considerations and issues that should be dealt with before the release. These are set out in Part 2 of this book. There is a lot to think about and plan for when setting up a release. The release checklist is a good starting point in order to ensure that you are on top of all of the pre-release tasks that you have.

Consistency is critical. The amount of work required to succeed can seem daunting, but if you do a little bit every day, you will move forward and can achieve great things. I actually set my most recent album cover as my laptop background. This forces me to think about the release all the time. You may have your own strategy, like stickies on your fridge or tasks set out in your Google calendar. Whatever it is, hopefully it will encourage you to ask yourself: Is there something else that I can do today to fulfill the goals set out in my plan? Do not be discouraged by the roadblocks that you will face. That is inevitable. Remember, slow and steady wins the race.

Chapter 11 Go after every revenue stream

It has been said that the music business is a business of pennies. And in many ways this is true. It is difficult to make a living from one revenue stream; it is the combination of revenues that can add up to a living. There is money to be made from many different sources – from your live performances, songs, recordings, name, and from your endorsement of products. Unfortunately, in order to get many of these fees and royalties, you have to be very diligent with paperwork.

The music industry is founded on various forms of intellectual property. Whether through copyright or trademark, most revenues flow from laws created by legislation and common law.

The *Copyright Act* of Canada (and related copyright acts around the world) creates two main copyrights that come into play in the music industry. One is the copyright in the composition or musical work and the other is the copyright in the sound recording. The Copyright Primer in Part 2 sets out the nature of these two copyrights as well as other related copyrights.

Your band or artist name is considered a "trade name". Trademarks and trade names are protected under the *Trade Mark Act* of Canada and under the common law right of "passing off". Personality rights (or the right to control your own image and persona) are also protected under common law.

The following chart is a synopsis of the revenues flowing from the copyrights in your songs, sound recordings, trademarks, trade name and personality rights. Over time, you may develop relationships with record labels, music publishers and merchandising companies to help finance and manage these revenue streams. However, in order to get to that point in today's music world, you will probably have to understand and deal with all of these issues yourself for some time. The further you are able to develop your own career, the better the deals that you will be able to make.

MUSIC BUSINESS REVENUES

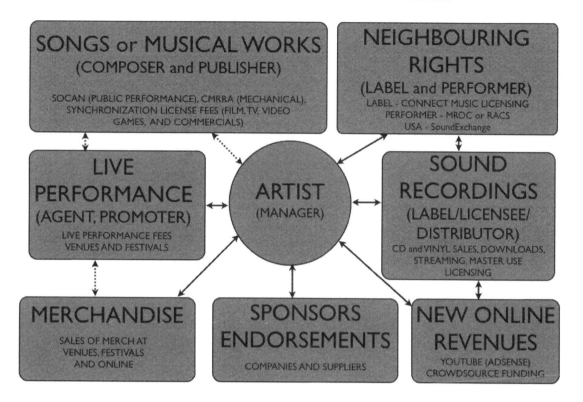

EXPLANATION OF CHART

Artist and Manager. The artist is at the centre of the chart. Most revenues flow from activities generated by the artist. The Manager works directly with the Artist and will act as the Artist representative in regard to most the revenue streams.

Live Performance is probably the largest revenue stream for Artists. This can account for up to 90% of an Artist's revenues including merchandise sales generated directly from live performances and touring. Live revenues normally consist of guarantees and /or a percentage of ticket and door sales.

Merchandise is a very important revenue for artists at all stages of an artist's career. Early on, this can be the revenue that puts gas in the van. As an artist grows, merch sales can become a massive part of overall Artist revenues whether through tours, website or stores.

Sponsorships and Endorsements. In many cases, sponsorships and endorsements have become a welcome addition to the revenue streams that an Artist can generate. Associating an Artist with a produce like Red Bull, MAC makeup, Gibson guitars and other products can be a win-win for

Artists and companies.

Publishing or revenues from songwriting or composition has also seen a decline on the mechanical license fee side due to record sale decreases. Public Performance revenues through radio and television are massive. Also, synchronization licensing for film, television, video games and commercials continues to be a very important source of revenue. See below for a more detailed discussion of music publishing revenues.

Sound recording revenues. While revenues from sound recordings are presently flatlining, they are still a significant source of revenue. Online sales and sales off the stage can generate a good revenue stream for artists. Licensing of masters for use in film, television, video games and commercials has become a huge source of master revenues. See below in this chapter for a more detailed discussion of sound recording revenues.

Neighbouring Rights revenues have been around for nearly two decades, but artists are still confused about these royalties. If an artist performs on a sound recording, then the performers are entitled to a royalty from the public performance of that sound recording including radio and at venues. An Artist needs to register lead or side performances with MROC or RACS/ACTRA in order to receive these royalties. The owner of the sound recording is also entitled to a neighbouring right royalty through Connect Music Licensing. If the Artist also owns the sound recording, then the Artist can apply for *both* the performance and the master royalties.

New revenues include registration with Adsense which allows the owner of a video (who has cleared all of the master and publishing rights) to receive payment for advertising on their Youtube channel. Also, crowdsource funding through platforms such as Kickstarter, Indiegogo and Pledgemusic has opened the door for artists to engage fans in directly supporting Artist projects.

REVENUES FROM SONGS OR MUSICAL WORKS

Song or Composition
Songwriter or Publisher
Copyright notice
(p) 2014 Publisher or Writer

Public Performance Royalties

SOCAN
(ASCAP/BMI/SESAC USA)

Radio
Television
Live
Online Streaming
(not downloads)

Reproduction Rights

Mechanical Licenses
for CD, Vinyl,
Download, Streaming

CMRRA
SODRAC
(Harry Fox Agency
USA)

Synchronization
Licensing

Film, Television,
Video Games,
Commercials

Sheet Music

Printed Scores
Charts
Folios
Online Sheet Music
Tabs
Lyric Sheets

Grand Rights

Music as part of
opera, musical, play
or other theatrical
performance

Direct Licensing

© 2014 WXYZ Publishing Inc. This is the copyright notice regarding the ownership of the underlying copyrights of the songs on the album. Initially the ownership rests with the author of the musical work, however the author may assign these copyrights to a publisher.

The above example assumes that the writer of the song has assigned the copyrights in his or her songs to a publishing company. This is referred to as a publishing deal.

Income flowing from this copyright:

Public Performance Royalties--Radio, Television, Theatrical, Live Performance and performance of pre-recorded songs. When a publisher signs up with SOCAN (the only body authorized to collect public performance royalties in Canada with some exceptions), the publisher agrees that it may only receive up to 50% of this revenue. The writer's share is paid directly to the writer (or in the case of a co-writer, royalties are split according to the writing percentages allocated for the song). A "work notification form" is filed with SOCAN to enable SOCAN to pay out royalties to the correct parties. This income is administered exclusively by SOCAN in Canada and primarily by ASCAP and BMI in the USA. Each country has its own public performance rights society to administer these revenues. The Canadian copyright board has watered down SOCAN's exclusivity by allowing broadcasters to secure a "modified blanket license" directly with film/television composers.

Mechanical Licensing Fees. If the song is reproduced on a "mechanical contrivance" such as a CD, cassette tape or other media, the Label or individual pressing such album pays the publisher/writer of the song a fee of approximately $0.083 per song per record sold. In Canada this is a "prescribed rate" set by agreement between the recording and publishing industry. In the USA, the rate is a "statutory rate" set by legislation. If an Artist or label wishes to record a song, they must first secure a "mechanical license" from the owner of the copyright. This can usually be done through the CMRRA in Canada and the Harry Fox Agency in the USA. If the writer is not represented by these agencies, then the Artist or label would have to contact the publisher or author of the work directly to secure such mechanical license. In the USA, once a song is publicly released, a mechanical license is automatically available for a statutory rate.

Synchronization licensing fees. When a song is placed on a film or T.V. soundtrack, the producer of the film or T.V. program is responsible for paying the publisher or author of the work a "Sync Fee". This fee is paid in order to allow the producer to synchronize the song to film. It is a similar concept to the mechanical license.

Ring tones and master tones. Use of songs on cell phones has become a lucrative business for music in some countries, but has never really caught on in North America.

Private Copying Levy. Owners of copyrights in musical works have been denied revenue due to pirating of copyrighted material for decades. Part VII of the Copyright Act creates the so-called "Blank Tape Levy" on recordable media including Cassette Tapes, CDs and other media as determined as commercially viable under the legislation.

Grand Rights. When musical works are used in theatrical shows or operas that combine the music with staging, dialogue and costuming, it is referred to as a "grand" right. These rights are not covered by SOCAN licensing and involve direct licensing between copyright holder and theatrical production company.

Private Copying Levy. The Private Copying Levy is paid to labels, performers, publishers and songwriters. If an artist is not published and not signed to a label, then it is important to register with the (a) Connect Music Licensing, (b) CMRRA or SODRAC, (c) SOCAN, and (d) RACS (ACTRA) or MROC.

Sheet Music and Folio sales. While this is another revenue stream for publishing, it is generally not a high-income area. This may change if sheet music can be seen as a "valued added" service to provide to the public. Also, online sheet music stores have been popping up and these may make sheet music sales viable again.

Grand Rights licensing fees. When a musical work is used as part of a dramatic or theatrical production, opera, ballet, musical or other such dramatic use, then the theatrical production company must obtain a "grand rights" license from the composer of the music. This will not apply to any "public domain" music such as musical works created by composers who passed away prior to 1960.

CPCC Member Collectives

There are a number of associations and agencies that collect royalties generated by copyright:

Canadian Musical Reproduction Rights Agency (CMRRA)
Society of Composers, Authors and Music Publishers of Canada (SOCAN) Society for Reproduction Rights of Authors, Composers and Publishers
in Canada (SODRAC)
Neighbouring Rights Collective of Canada (NRCC):
ACTRA Performers' Rights Society (RACS)
Société de gestion collective de l'Union des artistes inc. (ArtistI)
Musicians' Rights Organization Canada (MROC)
Connect Music Licensing (formerly AVLA)
Société collective de gestion des droits des producteurs de phonogrammes et de vidéogrammes du Québec (SOPROQ)

Types of deals associated with the copyrights in musical works

Publishing Deal. Under the Copyright Act, an author of a work may assign the underlying copyrights to a third party publisher. For many years a publisher took 100% of the copyrights in works for the life of the copyright in exchange for the writer receiving an advance against future royalties recouped against 50% of any revenues generated by the copyrights. After recoupment, the writer and the publisher would share 50/50 on all revenues. In regard to public performance royalties (SOCAN), the publisher under this deal would receive 50% of the public performance royalties (the so-called "publisher's share) and the writer would receive 50% of these royalties (the so-called "writer's share"). While these deal continue to exist, they are less common that Co-Publishing deals.

Co-Publishing Deal. More common today is the "co-publishing deal" where the writer retains 50% ownership of the copyrights in the work and receives up to 75% of the income generated by the copyrights. Having said that, the publisher normally takes 100% of the rights to administer the copyrights. The term is often for the life of the copyright in the musical work. It is possible to limit the term to, for example, be co-terminus (or to end) at the same time as an artist or license agreement.

Publishing Administration Deal. Another method of dealing with publishing is the publishing administration deal where the copyrights remain with the writer (s), but the publisher administers the publishing and charges a percentage commission for doing so (usually 15-25%). The term of these can range from one to five years (or more), often with renewal clauses.

Moral Rights. The author of the work may have retained his or her "moral" rights. Moral rights are the right to a "songwriting credit" and the right to maintain the "integrity" of the work (not to be used in a manner that would devalue the work, e.g. used in pornography or for a dog food commercial). "Moral rights" may be waived but not assigned, which mean that you cannot permanently give them away.

Copyright Registration. Formal registration is not legally required to protect copyright. Copyright in a work is protected automatically under the Copyright Act once the work is in a tangible or fixed form (such as a chart, sheet music or embodied in a sound recording). Notification as to the copyright (©) is not strictly required, but it is very important to give notice to the world as to the ownership of the underlying copyrights in a work: Radio stations will then know what publisher/writer to place on the reports to SOCAN; Film producers will then know what publisher/writer to place on the "cue sheet" to be registered with SOCAN; Artists wishing to use the song on other recordings will then know what entity to approach if they want to cover the song.

Copyright registration is not required, however if a composer's musical work is being released in any way in the USA, it is advisable to register copyrights with the Library of Congress. While there is an online registration for USA copyrights, Canadians are required to send in an actual copy of their CD as a foreign owner of copyright. This is a very economical and relatively easy registration option. In addition to having both the sound recording and musical works registered concurrently, this registration also opens the door to "punitive damages" in the USA for copyright infringement, which could be substantial depending on the nature of the infringement.

Canada also has a copyright registration system. You can go to: Canadian Copyright Registration and register each musical work title. Unlike the USA system, the Canadian Intellectual Property Office does not accept actual copies of musical works or sound recordings. This is not to be confused with the National Library, which requires the deposit of all sound recordings created in Canada, but does not offer any copyright registration protection.

MAPL. Canadian Content regulations set up by the CRTC. In order to qualify as Canadian Content for radio play on Canadian radio, recordings must have two of the four requirements. MAPL stands for "Music, Artist, Production and Lyrics". If a song qualifies (at least 2 of the 4 requirements), then it can be used by radio stations to fulfill their Canadian Content minimum play requirements. It is imperative that the MAPL logo filed be correctly placed on all commercial releases to ensure that radio stations are aware of Cancon status. Many commercial stations are mandated to play at least 35% Canadian Content. As a Canadian artist this gives the artist a distinct advantage in securing Canadian radio play.

Performance Revenue. It is critical that as a songwriter and performing artist that you file both "work notifications" (notifications to SOCAN as to your songwriting splits) and "live performance notifications" (written notice of your eligible live performances) with SOCAN. Live venues pay a flat fee license to SOCAN to play music. In order to get your share of this revenue, you have to file the live performance notification forms. The SOCAN work notification registrations will also ensure that you get paid for radio and television play. It may seem like a bother, but remember that this is a business of pennies and the pennies will add up.

If you are also involved with film or television music, whether as a composer or whether your music is being used as a cue in a scene, it is really important that you make sure that the songs used are properly filed with SOCAN by the producer. The CUE SHEET sets out the musical cues on any given TV episode or film.

Mechanical royalties were a revenue mainstay for composers while LP and CD sales were strong. As sales have dwindled, so have mechanical royalties. There is still a good revenue stream from iTunes sales and other online digital sales, but as streaming begins to take over with such services as Spotify, mechanical royalties will continue to decline. The CMRRA in Canada has been working hard to ensure that streaming companies pay their fair share of mechanical royalties. That is why Spotify and other such services are not available in Canada for the time being.

Film, Television and Video game syncs. Independent artists who own their songs and their sound recordings are in a particularly attractive position in regard to film, television and video game placements. The "music supervisors" who find music for film producers are able to come to you as a "one stop shop" meaning that they can clear all of the rights needed in one place. Also, the license fee that they can negotiate with you will often be lower than when they deal with a major label or large publishing company. Cultivating relationships with music supervisors could be huge for your career. In fact, and especially in the USA, music supervisors have become very powerful in becoming tastemakers for the public. The impact that some television placements have had on artist careers has been profound. That has made supervisors like Grey's Anatomy's Alexandra Patsavas very important indeed.

Grand Rights revenues can be very lucrative. If your music is used in a theatrical production, then the producers of the show need to secure a "grand rights license" to do so. Of course, if you composed the music for a show, there is a very good chance that you had to deal with this in the composer agreement. However, when shows use source music, they need to pay you from ticket sales. For example, if your music is used in a Cirque du Soleil show, then there would probably be an ongoing royalty payable while that show is running.

Sheet Music. Another area of revenue is sheet music and folios. When recording was in its infancy, sheet music was a key revenue stream. As sound recording, radio and other technologies grew, the demand for sheet music diminished. With the internet and increased online demands for "value added" products associated with artists growing, the possibility of generating revenues from sheet music may grow over the next few years.

REVENUES FROM MASTERS OR RECORDINGS

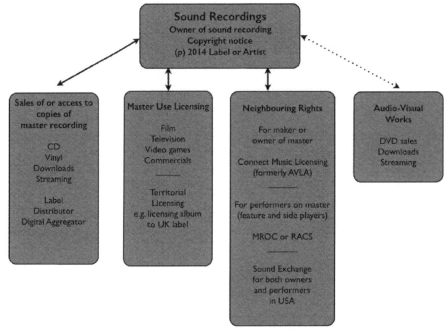

"Between 2000 and 2010, record store sales declined more than 76%" (Totalbankruptcy.com).

(p) 2014 ABCD Records Inc.. This is the copyright notification as to the owner of the copyrights in the "sound recording". This is usually a record label, however in the case of an independent Artist, the Artist may own such rights. Again, copyright registration is not required as it is automatic once the sound recording is in a fixed form, however the same registration issues may apply as set out above in musical works/songwriting.

Income generated from the sound recording:

For decades, the bread and butter revenue for the music industry – meaning the record labels and music publishers - was driven by record sales. The reason artists toured was to support album releases. Labels funded sound recording, touring and video production. That model has now flip-flopped. Other than Top 20 artists, CDs have really become a merch item along with t-shirts and posters. Tours are where the money is made.

Interesting fact: this has always been the case for artists. Bruce Allen, who manages Bryan

Adams and Michael Bublé, told me once that it has always been the live performances where the bulk of the revenues have flowed for artists. For now, it is still very important to manufacture CDs for sale on the road, but that may change over the next few years.

Record Sales Revenue. This includes revenues generated by direct sales and sales of records through third party distributors of physical product including Vinyl, CDs, Cassettes, DVDs, Data Sticks and other physical delivery mechanisms. Traditionally, labels or artists would distribute physical product to dedicated music retail stores. Most major retailers of physical music have disappeared. Over the past few years chains like HMV, A&B Sound, Sam the Record Man, Virgin and others have either downsized or closed entirely. This has led to many independent distributors closing down such as Fusion III, Festival Distribution and PHD Distribution. Major label distribution has downsized to the point that the majors have been forced to lay off tens of thousands of employees. The predominant consensus is that the massive prevalence of P2P and other free download sites has resulted in the collapse of the traditional recorded music industry. Even large recording artists are experiencing dramatic decreases in traditional sales. Ironically, music is more listened to than ever before in history.

In the event that an artist signs a typical old-school artist deal for traditional CD sales, the breakdown of revenue is normally as follows:

Retail Sale $14.99 Wholesale Price $10.00
To Label from Distributor $6.50
Mechanical Royalties to songwriters/publishers $0.81
Manufacturing $1.50
Artist royalties $1.00
Left for Label $3.19

It is interesting to note that major deals treat digital sales in the same way as traditional sales, even though there is no manufacturing, distribution or retail costs. Many independent labels have moved to overall revenue percentage splits or "net deals". The major trend is that as traditional sales have gone down, record labels have moved to so- called "360 deals" that get into live performance, merchandise, publishing and other revenue areas not traditionally open to labels.

In today's music market most independent artists make sales from physical product through:

  a. off-the-stage sales (treating CDs as merchandise); and
  b. sales through mail order and website driven sales.

Traditional retail store sales of physical product are now only a small part of anticipated revenues for recording artists. The advantage to independent artists is that the retailer, wholesaler and label are cut out of the picture and artists are able to make the lion's share of the revenue. Where under an artist deal, artists made about $1.00 per record recoupable against recording costs, now an artist can sell CDs for $10.00 and clear from $5.00-$6.00 net per CD after mechanical royalties, manufacturing and venue commissions. In this way an artist can make the same revenue from selling only a fifth of what they did under an artist deal. Artists with an established following may consider direct marketing as a profitable sales model.

Consider that many funding agencies require proof of sales in order to qualify for certain programs. Make sure that you check well in advance as to what is acceptable as a qualified proof of sale. Bands can register their off-the-stage sales with Soundscan, however there is an annual fee to do this.

Online Digital Sales. From the outset it is imperative that all artists/labels encode their masters with ISRC codes – received from Connect Music Licensing office for digital tagging of sound recordings (see below). This is required by all major online digital retailers i.e. iTunes, Puretracks, Napster to tracks sales online.

Sales through such models as $0.69/$0.99/$1.29 per track iTunes (up to now DRM protected tracks with limited transferability) have dominated the legitimate download arena. In fact, iTunes represents 95% of the overall digital sales revenue. The explosion of the iPod and related products by Apple Computers has driven this success. Also, the iStore, which is linked to the iPod software, has created sales like no other online retailer.

Unfortunately, the approximately $10 billion per annum worldwide loss in traditional sales has not been even remotely replaced by digital download sales. Most artists and label access the myriad online retailers, subscription services and mobile phone retailers through aggregators such as Tunecore, CD Baby and The Orchard. Aggregators usually charge a fee of between 9-15% of digital sales revenues and/or an up-front set-up charge.

Streaming Services. Pundits believe that the future music consumption model will be subscription based. The popularity of Netflix for the film and television community seems to be bearing that prediction out. While Spotify, Pandora and iTunes Radio are not available in Canada yet due to our streaming royalty rates, the movement to subscription based streaming models over download models may present significant further challenges to the online sales model. Rdio is the first major subscription service in Canada and it seems to be doing very well. The problem is that services like Spotify pay a fraction of a cent per stream. So far, royalties for many artists from streaming as reported through their aggregators have been negligible, however some labels are reporting some good revenues from these streaming music sites. In fact, Spotify claimed to have paid out half a billion dollars in royalties in 2013. There is no question that there is a movement towards this model and away from the paid download model. Over the next few years we shall see if the subscription based model allows for increased revenues for copyright creators and owners.

Territorial Master Use Licenses. This revenue stream involves licensing masters to third party labels to release records in specific territories such as Europe, Asia or Australia. Some territories, such as Japan and the U.K. still have a relatively strong traditional CD sales markets. In Tokyo, the last Tower Records retail store still thrives. In Japan, piracy is very rare. Statistically, while Canadian consumers pay for 1/50 downloads, in Japan it is about 1/1. There are opportunities in some countries for licensing deals, where an artist or label will license masters for an 18-22% of PPD – a wholesale base – usually about $1.70 - $2.00 per CD sold.

Compilation Master Use Licensing. Compilation CDs from film, television and specialty market CDs had a good run a few years ago. For some time, compilations sat at the top of retail charts. With the demise of traditional CD sales, compilations are less impactful than they have been. There are still, however, certain compilation series that remain popular. Normally, owners of the sound recording copyrights share pro rata with other tracks on compilations for royalties. These usually work out to from $0.10 - $0.20 per track. It is important to note that these licenses often include the right to sell through online retail stores, which may contravene exclusive distribution agreements with artist/label aggregators.

Film, Television and Video Game Master Use Licenses. Film, TV and video game producers require a master use license to use a sound recording on any audiovisual presentation. A film requires two licenses—the above mentioned "Sync License" from the publisher and a "Master Use License" from the label. These are flat fee licenses that range anywhere from gratis (free) to hundreds of thousands of dollars, depending upon the use and the stature of the artist. The licenses have become very important in the music industry, not only from a marketing point of view, but also a key income stream. In fact, placements on highly rated television shows can result in massive marketing boosts for artists. The show "Grey's Anatomy" was instrumental in launching many music careers. This phenomenon has also made music supervisors such as Alexandra Patsavas of Chop Shop Supervision some of the most powerful people in the music business.

As an independent artist you normally own both the copyrights in the record and the songs. This allows you to do "one stop" clearance of music for film, television and video games. This is very attractive to the music supervisors who source all of this music. While the market is very competitive, supervisors are out at conferences and festivals and can be approached. If you can create a relationship with a supervisor, there is a chance that they will help you place your music. Make sure that you understand how each supervisor likes to receive music for consideration. Never send emails with attachments. Links to a Dropbox or Box folders are best. Stay away from sites like Hightail (formerly YouSendIt) as these generally have time limits on them. Supervisors may file away your email for months and come back to it. Some supervisors still want physical CDs. Again, find out what they want to receive and how they want to receive it.

Make it easy for supervisors by outlining the beats per minute, the genre, description (e.g. male vocal rock), sounds like (this is always a tough one), who owns the copyrights and your contact information. Put "one stop clearance" on all submissions. Be patient. It can take months or even years to get the right chance to get a good placement.

If you get an offer, be easy to deal with and quick. These deals need to be done often within minutes. That means that someone in your band or your team has to have the right to sign-off on sync and master use deals. That should be set out clearly in your band agreement. I have run into situations where artists cannot find a co-writer or are out of town or simply cannot be found and big deals fall through.

Neighbouring Rights. After 24 years as a copyright lawyer, I've noticed the Neighbouring Rights granted to owners of copyrights in sound recordings and performers on those recordings still seem to be a mystery for many artists. This is a right created under the *Copyright Act*. Broadcasters are responsible to pay a tariff to approved collection agencies in order to compensate the performers on records and the labels owning the sound recordings. Established in 1997, Re:Sound is an umbrella collective that collects a percentage of advertising revenue (as mandated by the Copyright Board), from various users of sound recordings in Canada . Re:Sound has relationships with other organizations to distribute the Neighbouring Rights royalties. Connect Music Licensing administers Neighbouring Rights for Labels (or the makers or owners of sound recordings – which could be an artist) and RACS/ACTRA or MROC administer the performer's rights. If an artist is the owner of the copyright in a sound recording as well as the performer, then the artist should apply for these royalties through Connect Music Licensing and through the performers side.

The USA has a limited Neighbouring Right for digital performance royalties (satellite radio, internet radio and cable TV music channels). This is administered by SoundExchange. So, if you are being played on Sirius, XFM or Digital Cable in the USA, you should sign up with SoundExchange.com. SoundExchange is an independent, nonprofit performance rights organization that is designated by the U.S. Copyright Office to collect and distribute digital performance royalties for featured recording artists and sound recording copyright owners, (usually a record label) when their sound recordings are performed on digital cable and satellite television music, internet and satellite radio (such as XM and Sirius). SoundExchange currently represents over 3,500 record labels and over 31,000 featured artists and whose members include both signed and unsigned recording artists; small, medium and large independent record companies; and major label groups and artist-owned labels.

USA tax treaty. Please note that for any dealings with USA based services you will need to apply to the IRS in the USA for what is called an EIN number (EIN number online application). Acquiring an EIN number allows you to receive royalties generated in the USA with no withholding tax. you have a deal involving the receipt of royalties directly from a USA based company, you will be required to fill out want is called a W8BEN FORM and send that to the USA company in order to comply with IRS requirements and the Canada/USA Tax treaty. Unfortunately, until you have gone through this process, USA based companies will usually not be able to send you any payment or at the very minimum will have to hold back royalties for US tax withholding.

Private Copying Levy. Owners of copyrights in sound recordings have been denied revenue due to pirating of copyrighted material for decades. Part VII of the Copyright Act created the so-called "Blank Tape Levy" on recordable media including Cassette Tapes, CDs and other media determined as commercially viable under the legislation. There has been a lot of controversy surrounding this levy. A proposal by the Copyright Board to institute a tariff on digital audio devices was struck down by the Federal Court of Appeal and the new Copyright Act amendments failed to extend the Private Copying Levy to hard drives and mobile music devices. Over time, this levy revenue will dwindle and eventually disappear.

What is the ISRC? (from Connect Music Licensing website)

The ISRC (International Standard Recording Code) is the international identification system for sound recordings and music video recordings. Each ISRC is a unique and permanent identifier for a specific recording, which can be permanently encoded into a product as its digital fingerprint. Encoded ISRC provide the means to automatically identify recordings for royalty payments.

The ISRC system is the key to royalty collection for recordings in the digital information age. ISRC is a unique, reliable, international identification system and provides a unique tool for the purpose of rights administration. ISRC is a useful identification tool in the electronic distribution of music. ISRC coding is compatible with standards developed in the field of consumer electronics and is readable by hardware already used in the recording industry.

ISRC is cost effective - it can be put into operation without requiring special investment in equipment or technologies. The ISRC consists of twelve characters representing country (2 characters), registrant (3 characters), year of reference (2 digits) and designation (5 digits). It is divided into four elements separated by hyphens and the letters ISRC should always precede an ISRC code.

What kind of deals are associated with the sound recordings?

Artist Deal. A recording artist may sign an Artist deal with a record label. In this case, the Artist will usually assign all master recording and recording performance copyrights to the record label. The label pays for all costs of recording, pressing, promotion and marketing (including video production). The label will often pay an advance against future royalties with a royalty rate of 10-13% of retail selling price. So-called "net deals" are quite common now, where labels split any profits with Artists 50/50.

Licensing Deal. If the artist records his or her own masters, the artist may license such recordings to a third party label. The label is not responsible for the costs of production in this case, but do take on the costs of pressing, marketing and promotion (video production would probably rest with the Artist). The Label will usually pay an advance against royalties with a royalty rate of 15-18% of retail selling price. Again, 50/50 net deals are beginning to materialize for licensing.

Distribution Deal. The artist who produces his or her own masters may release directly. In this case, the artist becomes the de facto record label. The artist is responsible for all costs of production, pressing, marketing and promotion. The artist will likely have a distribution deal with a third party distributor, of which pays a wholesale price of $7.00-$9.00 per CD sold. Out of this, the artist takes care of all costs to do with pressing, marketing and promotion.

Digital Aggregators. Artists and Labels often release digitally now through aggregators such as Tunecore, CD-Baby or The Orchard, which allows them access to such internet download stores as iTunes, Napster and Puretracks. Revenues vary, however the iTunes model is $0.69/$0.99/$1.29 per download. The retailer usually takes a percentage and the aggregator takes a percentage of this net amount. Generally, on a digital sale, a label/Artist will make approximately $0.55 per track out of which the mechanical royalty at $0.083 must be paid to the owners of the copyrights in the musical work.

360 Deals. The decline in traditional CD sales has lead to record companies having to expand the revenue streams that they are able to access. Over the last five years, the number of so-called "360 Deals" has risen dramatically. These deals can originate from any source – management, producer, studio, label, publisher and others. This has muddied the waters in terms of the roles that each of these members of your team would have traditionally played. The 360 Deal normally takes a percentage from every revenue stream (hence the 360 degree deal)– including live, recording, publishing, merchandise, and endorsements. The problem is that many of these companies know that they need the revenue, but are not necessarily ready, willing or able to carry out the actual role that goes along with such acquiring such rights. For example, a manager signing an artist to a 360 deal may be great on the live side, but that manager may not know the first thing about administering publishing rights. Some companies have taken the model to heart and have built teams to deal with all of the rights that they have acquired. Some newer labels have adapted to the new music business paradigm and succeeded. For example, Arts & Crafts is a great example of a label and management company that often acquires "360" rights, but also works all of those rights to great success.

If presented with this kind of deal or any other significant deal it is imperative that you engage a very good music lawyer.

REVENUES FROM TRADEMARKS, TRADENAMES AND PERSONALITY RIGHTS – THE IMPORTANCE OF YOUR NAME AND BRAND

What is in a name? Well in music, it is everything. Think of the KISS or AC/DC brands. They are worth millions and millions of dollars. Protecting and nurturing these brands is an essential part of sustaining a career in music. Long after record sales have plateaued, merchandise sales can continue to grow.

A good example of the power in a name is the band "Yes". This progressive rock band, which started in the 1970s, developed a huge following. Over the years, the members of the band changed, leaving Chris Squire, the bass player, with the control of the name. When the original members of the band wanted to do a reunion tour, they were unable to do so because Chris Squire did not approve the tour. The band recorded and toured as Anderson Bruford Wakeman Howe (which sounded more like an accounting firm than a rock band). Even with the Trevor Rabin-led commercial success of Yes, this new brand was simply not as popular. This group could only fill venues half the size of Yes. Same music. Same members. Different name. When Yes went out in later years under the Yes banner, they packed arenas again. Hmm…. The moral of this story is that you need to understand how important your band name is, not only for building a brand, but also in representing who you are to the public. So, make sure you have a very clear band agreement.

Understanding your rights in regard to your name and/or logo is a good idea. There are two ways that your rights can arise: (a) through the common law right of "passing off" and (b) through registration under the *Trade-Mark Act*. Many new and emerging artists cannot afford to register trade names through the Canadian Intellectual Property Office (can cost $2000-4000 and take over two years for a Canada only registration, USA registration can be $5,000+), but are very concerned about other artists using their name. This is a very common issue.

Before the legislation, a body of law developed in England called the law of "passing off". This law developed under UK "tort" law and by extension was adopted by Canadian law. Basically, this gives you the right to sue for damages suffered through the unauthorized use of an unregistered trademark. When you use your name, you are developing "good will" in that name. "good will" is the intangible value that your name develops over time. If someone uses your established name, then they are misrepresenting themselves as you and you can take action for this. In order to do that you need to establish that:

1) you own the "good will";
2) there has been a misrepresentation by a third party; and
3) the misrepresentation caused damage to your good will.

If you cannot afford registration, then it is very important that you establish evidence that you actually own the name. Unfortunately, this is really done on a territory-by-territory basis. Simply registering a URL or releasing your songs throughout the world on iTunes is not in itself enough to establish ownership of the name. Ideally, you can actually tour in different provinces and countries in order to establish your name. Keep copies of press as evidence. If you can get radio play or sales in different territories, this is further evidence that you are establishing your name.

The first thing you need to do is search through the internet for other bands or artists with your name. If there is a band anywhere that is using it, you may want to consider another name. If the band in question is small and isolated to a specific territory, you need to weigh this with the fact that they have probably established some ownership in that territory and that might block you from using it in that territory. This can become maddening once you have spent years building up your name. Having to change your name mid-stream can really set you back in terms of notoriety.

If you have established your name in a territory and you get notice of another artist using that name, then you must be vigilant in protecting your rights. This means acting right away. Don't wait for a year and then try and send a cease and desist letter. You may be giving the artist using your name an opening to challenge you.

If you have registered your trademark, then your rights to go after people using your name are based on infringement of your rights as established under the Act. It is a different type of proceeding, as registration gives exclusive rights and a clear ownership right, whereas non-registration common law rights are based on misrepresentation. In other words, you are better off registering, but if you can't afford it at least there are some common law rights that you can rely on.

Personality Rights

As a recording artist it is important to recognize the importance of your rights as an individual to exploit your name and likeness. While band names generally fall in the area of trademark/ passing off law, individual artist rights have developed out of privacy law.

The use of an artist's likeness includes images on film, television, videos, posters, t-shirts and any other public display of the Artist's image. This right to control the "publicity" and "personality" around one's name flows from privacy laws and the laws of "passing off". These rights developed both in common law and through legislation must be diligently protected as they represent a significant source of revenue for an Artist through merchandising, commercial endorsements, personal appearances, images in film and other public displays.

The right that we are discussing is commonly known as the "Right of Publicity". This right includes your right to control the commercial use of your name and likeness or clear aspects of your individual identity. As a property right, this will extend past the death of the person, e.g. Elvis. Another aspect of this right is the "Right to Privacy", which gives you the right to be left alone and the right to grant permission for public use of your personality.

The law in this area is continually developing and changing and can vary from country to country. It is, however, important to be aware of the fact that you do have a right to publicity around your name and the commercialization of your name, image and personality.

Chapter 12 Perseverance

The press loves an "overnight success" story. The reality is that most overnight success stories are actually 10 years in the making. The music business is about being ready to work hard for a sustained period without losing faith in your vision. That is the hardest part of trying to make a career in music. Most people simply cannot sustain a life living on Kraft dinner without throwing in the towel at some point. You need talent, but just as important is the willingness to stay the course no matter what.

Going back to Chapter 1, you really need to understand the role that you want to take in the music business. Do you really want a life as a recording artist, touring around the world and living out of a suitcase? If that is your dream, then perseverance is going to be a big part of this. If you have a burning desire to share your music live with a large audience, then this is a worthwhile dream of which you can go after. This is possible, but you have to be patient, driven and organized.

Huey Lewis and the News became massive in the 1980s. The real story however lies behind the scenes in the struggles that the band faced over many years. There were many incarnations of the band in San Francisco and in the UK in the 1970's. The band's first album in 1980 tanked. The second record "Picture This" did much better going gold, however with a delay in the release of the third record, the band was still performing small club dates. But they would not quit, and relentless touring led to huge radio success, which then pushed them into the stratosphere. From that point until the end of the 1980's, they became one of the biggest touring acts in the world. Their story is one of hard work and determination. Despite having many reasons to quit, they persevered and in the end, won. Their journey to success took 15 years.

Another great example of perseverance is Dan Mangan. Dan has literally won over one fan at a time through many years and has built a very loyal and appreciative base of support. At Music BC, we often use Dan as an example of how to succeed as an independent artist. He is talented, personable, hard working, well spoken and driven. He certainly understands where he fits in the music landscape and has continued to grow as a performer, writer and recording artist. Dan has also worked hard to build relationships within the music industry and most of the people I know would gladly help him out if asked. He gives more than he expects in return.

On the other hand, I have also dealt with a lot of bitter artists over the years. Obviously, there is only room at the very top for a handful of artists. Remember to understand your role in the business and embrace it. Understand that your path may take you in many different directions. Celebrate your successes, no matter how small. I remember seeing an interview with Pete Townshend from The Who. He was asked if there was anything he would have changed when he looks back on it all. He said that he would have enjoyed the ride a lot rather than having been such a grumpy bastard (or something like that). When you are in the moment, you don't always see the magic. Enjoy the journey and accept that each experience, good and bad, allows you to grow and develop as an artist. Those memories may become some of your fondest.

I often see the music business as a giant brick wall. You are handed a guitar pick and expected to somehow carve your way through to the other side. Keep chipping at that wall and you will get a splinter of cement, then a wedge, and eventually a brick will come loose. It can seem like you are getting nowhere, but every little thing that you do, every day adds up to a chance for success. Never forget that.

When promoting myself as an artist I get up every day and say to myself, "What am I going to do for my music career today?" I am not talking about conquering the world over night. I am talking about taking baby steps and always moving forward toward the goals that you set for yourself. If you do that, you can succeed. You can have a career in this difficult business. Polite persistence. Relationship building. Great songwriting and recording. Amazing live shows that grow and grow. An online presence that is active and engaging.

Conclusions

As you can see, there isn't just one thing that you must do to make a career in music. It is a combination of many elements combining together to create a career. The challenge is to find your gaps and fill them. There are undoubtedly steps in this book that you have already mastered and steps that you have not. Other steps, like songwriting, will be a lifelong journey. Strive to reach the following goals:

12 STEPS TO BUILDING A CAREER IN MUSIC:

1. You are clear as to your role in the music business and the roles of all of the members of your band are clearly defined.
2. You are willing to write, re-write and dig deep on all of your songs in order to make them truly great. You are committed to life-long growth as a songwriter.
3. You ensure that your sound recordings stand up against all artists in your genre. You are not satisfied with anything but top notch production.
4. Your professional materials are world-class, including demos, pictures, bios, website, videos.
5. You understand that you have to continually work on your live performance in order to make it impactful for all of your audiences.
6. You are willing to tour and showcase constantly in order to create a career in music.
7. You are active and engaging with social media such as Twitter, Facebook and YouTube and you constantly update your website.
8. You understand that a good relationship with the media is crucial.
9. You understand that you are an entrepreneur and treat your music career as a business.
10. You have a business plan to help to aide in your success and you prepare marketing plans for your tours and releases.
11. You learn everything that you can about copyright and revenues from music and exploit all the revenue streams that are out there.
12. You recognize that success in music is a long game and that you will stay the course no matter what.

Revisit this list of goals from time to time to make sure that you are on track. Good luck with your chosen role in the business. No matter what you choose, it is a difficult, yet rewarding path.

Follow your heart and stay true to your artistic vision, but never forget that this is a business. Empower yourself so that you can make your own good luck.

One final thought to leave you with. Treat everyone around you well. You never know where people will end up. The guy you know today working in the stock room at a major label could be a Vice-President of that same company in the future. The longer you are in the business, the smaller it gets. Over a career, you will need friends through the ups and downs. And people like to help their friends.

Part 2: Down the rabbit hole

Introduction

Part 2 of this book drills down into a few of the key issues presented in Part 1 "the 12 step program". First, I provide a summary of the Canadian *Copyright Act* with a discussion of the recent changes to the Act introduced by Bill C-11. Second, I provide outlines and notes of the preparation of both Business and Marketing plans. Then, I give you a release checklist. While this is not exhaustive, the checklist gives you an idea of the actions that you should be taking well prior to the release of your music to the public. Finally, I post the questions that you should be able to answer when preparing a band agreement. Ideally, you should have a written and signed band agreement that deals with all of the issues set out in that section of the book.

Chapter 1 Copyright Law in Canada

The Copyright Act is a federal act in Canada that creates and administers copyrights. The Act protects original works of authorship, including musical works (songs and compositions), sound recordings, performances (players on recordings) as well as literary, dramatic and artistic works amongst other rights. Under this Act, your rights continue for 50 years from the death of the creator of the work (see below).

Your rights under the Copyright Act

With some exceptions, if you hold or own a copyright, you have the exclusive right to produce, reproduce, perform, publish and alter the work. You may allow a third party to copy your work. You may also assign rights in your copyright to another person or a company e.g. publishing deal.

Moral rights

Very important rights set out in the act are your "moral rights". The creator or author of the work protected under the act has the right to the integrity of the work. This means that you have the right to stop the work from being changed or used in a way that could diminish the value and/or reputation of the work, e.g. use in an adult film or use by a political party. You also have the right to be associated with the work or to get a credit for your work. Moral rights may not be assigned but may be waived in whole or in part. Moral rights for a work exist for the same term as the copyright in the work.

Types of works protected by copyright

Copyright applies to all original works. For example:

Literary works - this would include lyrics (printed without the music), liner notes and other written materials created in support of sound recordings and songs.

Dramatic works - this would include all of an artist's film and video footage and audiovisual recordings.

Musical works - compositions that consist of both words and music or music only (note that lyrics without music fall into the literary works category). This is about songwriting and not the sound recording – sound recording is a separate and distinct copyright.

Artistic works - album artwork, band photographs, posters and other artwork created for or by the artist is copyrighted.

Performer's performance - performers such as actors, musicians, dancers and singers have copyrights in their performance. This is important for musicians and singers as their performance on a sound recording has its own copyright and must be assigned – even if a third party owns sound recordings, they cannot release a sound recording without an assignment or license of the performer's rights. As an extension of this right, the Copyright Act has created a so-called "neighbouring right" in performance, which allows the maker (record label) and performers on sound recordings to receive royalties for radio play in the same way as songwriters do.

Communication signals - broadcasters have copyrights in the communications' signals that are broadcast.

Sound recordings - "makers" of recordings, such as digital recordings, phonograph records and compact discs, which are called "sound recordings" in the Copyright Act, are also protected by copyright.

What is not protected:

Copyright only applies to an idea once it has been expressed in some fixed format. This includes making a chart or recording a song – this does not include writing a song without creating some fixed format to express it. If it is only in your head, then it is not copyrighted.

Title, names and factual information are not usually protected by copyright. They are part of the public domain.

Musical Works or Sound Recordings whose term of copyright have run are considered public domain. Public Domain works or recordings may be used without having to license such works. It is important to note that if an artist is covering a public domain song and arranges that song, then SOCAN and CMRRA will recognize a copyright in the arrangement and allow for part royalties to be paid. This is to recognize the new creation expressed in the arrangement.

Length of copyright term.

The term of copyright is measured by the life of the creator plus 50 years. In the case of a co-write, the copyright extends for 50 years from the death of the last remaining co-writer. For sound recordings, photographs and videos, copyright extends for 50 years from the date of the recording. Works enter the public domain when the term of copyright has expired. Public domain means that there is no further need to get licenses, as the original creator no longer has exclusivity over the work.

Please note that different jurisdictions have different length of terms for copyright. If an artist plans to cover a song, then the law defaults to the country of origin. For example, if you are covering an UK artist's song, then there is a good chance that UK copyright law will apply.

Automatic protection

Copyright protection exists as soon as an original work is created in a fixed form including the creation of a score, a music chart or recording of the song.

Please note that while copyright is automatic once in a fixed form, it is advisable to always put the following copyright notice on all recordings and printed materials:

(p) 2013 Blue Records Inc. (this is the owner of the copyright in the sound recording – this can be the artist or the record label)

© 2013 White Publishing Inc. (this is the owner of the copyright in the musical works – this can be the writers, the publisher or both in the case of co-publishing)

If the artist has not assigned its copyrights to a company, then copyrights are normally owned as follows:

(p) 2013 The Artist Name (an artist with more than one member is normally considered a partnership under the Partnership Act of BC – usually the band owns the copyrights in the sound recordings if the band paid for them)

(p) 2013 The Songwriters (the names of the actual songwriters would be placed here – often this is one or two members of a band, or a co-write with a third party producer or songwriter)

Please note that there is also a copyright in your artwork and it is advisable to put a copyright notice on any posters, inserts, CD covers and other printed materials:

© 2013 The Artist's Name or Photographer or Designer (whoever retains the copyright)

Recent changes to Copyright Act

The Act has just gone through a major overhaul to try and bring copyright into the new digital age and to honour Canada's commitment to international treaties (WIPO) on copyright. The USA has had legislation for some time dealing with digital media issues. The Digital Millennium Copyright Act (USA Digital Copyright) was the USA response to the explosion of digital media. Many feel that it tends to be too aggressive in protecting copyright. For example, the "notice and take down" provisions (where notice of a copyright infringement puts the onus on the web host to take down the alleged infringement. It is often stated that this does not allow for due process and is open to abuse). The Canadian response has been long over-due.

Bill C-11 was a very important document for ensuring that Canada's laws become current in light of the explosion of digital technology and our international treaty obligations. The bill was brought into law in 2012. Unfortunately, there are some serious concerns with the new revisions:

Fair dealing

Fair Dealing in Canada has developed over a long period of time. Fair Dealing provisions in the *Copyright Act* create exceptions to copyright when a copyrighted work is used for research, private study, criticism, review or news reporting. Bill C-11 has now extended these exceptions by allowing a copyrighted work to be used for education, parody or satire. These new exceptions have not been tested in the courts, so there is some uncertainty at present as to how these Fair Dealing provisions will be applied. The parody and satire exception has been available in the USA for many years. While USA precedent has no direct impact on Canadian law, it is quite possible that Canadian courts will look to the USA experience from some guidance in making decisions in that regard.

Non-commercial users. The so-called "mash-up" provision. This allows internet users to post content that they create using existing copyrights e.g. editing home videos to Bryan Adams music and posting on YouTube. While the government is trying to allow innocent consumers to use the internet without undue restrictions, this section opens a door that is unprecedented in the world. The "non-commercial user" language is vague and could potentially lead to the devaluation of musical copyrights. Notwithstanding the sections attempt to balance some of the copyrights (no individual may cause "substantial damage" to the work) the use of unlicensed music in this manner with no clear enforcement mechanism may lead to the devaluing of copyrights and an abuse of creators moral rights.

Notice and Notice provisions. The Canadian response to the USA "notice and take down". If a site is given notice of an infringement, then the site has a duty to give notice to the infringer. There is no obligation to stop or take down the copyright infringement. The independent music sector is made up of individual entrepreneurs and small businesses. The section as drafted, places an unreasonable burden on these copyright holders to enforce their copyrights. It is impractical to expect copyright owners to go to court every time there is an infringement notice. The copyright infringer will continue to infringe with impunity knowing that there is very little chance that copyright owners will have the resources to come after them for such actions. We had hoped to create a fair, robust and equitable provision that provides protection for Internet Service Providers ("ISPs") while allowing for the notice and take down of illegally posted intellectual property. The provision will come into force January 2015.

Statutory damages. This section caps infringement damages for non-commercial users at $5000.0. In the same vein as above, the capping of statutory damages for individuals may make the payment of damages the "cost of doing business" on the internet. Individuals and small business copyright owners will look at the cost of litigation vs. the limited damages and decide that litigation is impractical. Further, even if there is a judgment, it will be too small to have any real impact on infringers. Again, copyright infringers may infringe with impunity. In fact, the provisions of this section will create a virtual vehicle for licensing of infringement.

Ephemeral Rights. Radio stations have been paying a "broadcast mechanical tariff" for the transfer of data to their station databases. This is also called an "ephemeral right". Radio broadcasters have fought hard and continue to fight to have this provision removed. The new provision allows broadcasters to possibly avoid the tariff if they do not keep digital files more than 30 days. If broadcasters are able to find a technical way to allow the digital music files to be considered "temporary," then they may well be able to avoid the requirement to pay this "broadcast mechanical tariff". If that happens, this would lead to a reduction of revenue to the music industry of approximately $21.2 Million per year. Revenues in the music industry have been steadily declining over the past ten years leading to a crisis in the business. In a time where the music industry needs support, these new revisions may further erode the revenue streams required to sustain the music business.

Royalty exemption. Section 68.1 (1) (a) (i) of the Copyright Act created a $1.25 million exemption for the first advertising revenues of commercial radio station prior to the payment of neighbouring rights royalties (there is no exemption for public performance royalties). This provision was created in order to facilitate the transition to a new royalty many years ago and simply does not apply today. This exemption was not removed with the new provisions and $7 million in possible new revenue to the industry was lost.

Private Copying Levy. The industry has repeatedly requested that the private copying levy be extended to hard drives and portable music devices storing pirated music. This extension was not brought into law, meaning that Private Copying Levy revenues will decline and die over time (as they are only on CDs and Cassette Tapes).

Educational materials. The new revisions allow for the printing of copyrighted materials for educational use without compensation to the creators or owners of copyrights. Educational book publishers and creators see these changes as a serious erosion of creator's copyrights. In fact, the textbook business is now facing a major collapse. This would presumably also apply to sheet music of existing copyrighted works that are used for educational purposes.

Digital Locks. Any technological measure designed to access or copy a copyrighted work cannot be circumvented, including musical works and sound recordings.

Internet Service Providers (e.g. TELUS, Rogers or Shaw) are not liable for copyright infringement. This is a blanket exemption for ISPs from liability for copyright infringement. While many critics feel that this is unacceptable, it does comply with international treaty obligations.

New Exclusive Rights

The following new exclusive rights have been added for the benefit of copyright owners: A copyright owner now has explicit "first distribution rights", i.e. for a tangible work, the exclusive rights to sell or otherwise transfer ownership of the work, as long as that ownership has never previously been transferred in or outside Canada, with the authorization of the copyright owner. This extends to performers and makers of sound recordings, in the case of first sale or distribution of a tangible CD or DVD.

Performers and makers of sound recordings also have the exclusive right to control the online transmission of sound recordings, i.e. to make a sound recording available to the public over the Internet in a way that allows a member of the public to have access to such sound recording from a place and time individually chosen by the member of the public.

Length of copyright

We had hoped to have the length of copyright in all areas be increased from 50 to 70 years in order to maintain parity with other jurisdictions, but this did not happen.

Chapter 2

Business Plans

A Business Plan is the overall plan and strategy for a project or company. A Marketing Plan is a component of a Business Plan or a stand alone document for a particular activity e.g. record release or tour. The Business Plan is very useful for focusing in on how an artist or music company plan to achieve success in the music industry. It sets out the basic structure of the project or company and what steps need to be taken to achieve some set goals. The plan also proposes timelines and financial forecasts to help set realistic goals. Investors and lenders often require a Business Plan prior to investing or lending funds. While it may seem like a daunting experience, creating a Business Plan for your project or music company is one of the best ways to reach the level of success that you want to achieve.

BUSINESS PLAN TEMPLATE

TITLE PAGE
INDEX

Executive Summary

This should set out in no more than one page the overall plan. The reader should be able to get the gist of the entire business plan from this section. Often, it is best to leave this exercise until the end of the process.

Mission Statement

This is a summary of the aims and values of the company. It is a good idea to figure out what you plan to achieve with your music business venture. You may also want to think about things like what kind of funding you will or will not go after. For example, some companies will not take funding from cigarette companies.

Company /Partnership Overview

This gives you a chance to set out how your organization is set up. Are you a limited company? Who are the shareholders? Are you a partnership? Do you have a partnership agreement?

Market and Products

How are you going to make money in music? What are you going to sell? This includes everything from live performance, to merch, to CDs, to online sales, to publishing.

Objectives

Products and Services Description

Set out in detail what you plan to sell and in what form.

History and Current Status

Give your history and what you have achieved so far with your various revenues from the music business.

Proprietary Rights

This refers to who owns the copyrights and the trademarks associated with your music. If you are an indie artist, you probably own your sound recordings, your music publishing and your trade name/band name.

Industry and Marketplace Analysis Industry analysis.

The music business has gone through so me profound changes over the past 10 years. Showing you r understanding of the challenges and opportunities is important.

Marketplace analysis

Show an understanding of your marketplace. Where are you touring? Where are you selling music?

Consumer Analysis

Demographics are critical. Understanding your audience and fan base is the starting point for all of your marketing. It drives all of your marketing plans. How old are your fans? What sex are they predominantly? Where do they live?

Competitor Analysis

In today's global digital world, you are not only competing with your peers, but also all artists in your genre. Understanding this and recognizing how competitive your market is can be vital.

Marketing Strategy (see marketing plan discussion below)

Product and service strategy Branding and Art design Online strategy
Radio
Music videos
Touring

Club Promotions Publicity strategy Advertising
Film and television placements Special markets
Monitoring techniques

Producing the Music

How do you plan to produce the music? Lay out your recording plan in detail.

Artist Signing Projects

Are you planning to sign other artists to your "label" or is this a single purpose company? Anthem Records was set up for RUSH because no one would sign them. When they proved everyone wrong that label went on to sign a lot of other artists. If you are focused on your project only, that is perfectly fine, but set it out.

Third Party Projects

Again, will you be working on third party projects or is 100% of the focus on your own act?

Distribution and Manufacturing

How are you planning to get your music out? Would you like to get a distributor or are you happy with using an aggregator like TuneCore, CD Baby or The Orchard/IODA and sell off the stage? Are you pressing vinyl?

Artist Management

Do you have management? If not, what is your plan about management in the future? Company Organization

How is the company set up? Who are the executives – president, secretary, and treasurer? Have you created a special class of shares for investors?

Company Management Team

Who is going to do what in your company?

Administrative Staff

Can you afford staff? If not, have you considered interns? Some bands have been very successful in using interns from music business schools to help with their marketing and business.

Legal, Accounting and Bookkeeping

Every company needs bookkeeping, accounting and legal. Make sure that you have this in place early on. Showing this in your plan will instil confidence in any investors that you might be going after.

Timeline

Set out the key milestones for success that you plan to achieve:

Funding applications
Songwriting and pre-production
Production
Single releases
Album Release date
Touring plans

Summary of financials

Financial Statements – revenues/expenses and cash-flow projections

You may need help from an accountant for this part. More complex financials include balance sheets and income statement projections. If you can't afford the expense, then you should at least set out a cash-flow analysis on a spreadsheet. You can set out all of the possible revenues over a three-year period and the expenses that you will incur during that period. Of course, your expenses are going to be bigger in the beginning and then over time you should flip into a profitable situation. Be reasonable and realistic in your forecasting.

Chapter 3

Marketing Plan

One of the most important business activities is developing marketing plans for your releases and tours. Many artists create marketing plans for funding agencies, but these are not meant to be "real". I challenge artists to create actual marketing plans that you can use to set up releases and tours. Making a plan will help you to keep focused and to streamline your activities. Many artists simple react to situations and put out fires instead of creating a clear path to achieve their goals. In fact, a plan can take a lot of pressure off of a band - knowing what you are going to do in advance is a great way to reduce stress.

Marketing Plan Template

[INSERT COVER PAGE PICTURE OR ARTIST PICTURE AND ARTIST NAME]

General:

A marketing plan can be used for part of a FACTOR application, setting up a tour, outlining the rollout of a CD or digital release, or it can form part of a bigger business plan for financing or investors. It is important to ensure that a marketing plan is drafted with the reader in mind. What is the purpose of the marketing plan?

As far as the look and feel of the marketing plan, it may be of value to consider adding pictures and graphics to help emphasize points and bring a sense of excitement to the plan.

Always try and be specific about the artist's goals (don't generalize) and be realistic (don't set out goals that are unattainable).

Topic headings that you should consider adding to a marketing plan: Bullets off the top could include:

- Artist
- Distributor
- Release
- Date
- Format
- Genre
- Target market (Very important for establishing focus of marketing strategy)

Biography

The first thing that an artist needs to do is tell the reader who they are. What is the artist's background? Where did they come from? What have they achieved so far? Are there any highlights that could be emphasized – awards, charting, tour support positions?

Live Performance

Bill Gates recently stated in his book his adherence to John Naisbitt's "High Tech, High Touch" theory. The music application of this theory is the use of the internet to promote yourself while on tour. Your plan in regards to the personal connection with your fans through live performance is equally as important as your plan to develop an effective online strategy.

In the past, touring was not as essential as it is now. In many ways, we have reverted to the pre-MTV era where bands had to get out and connect with fans one at a time. Bands must get out on the road to build their base. The days of relying on a TV-based video to launch a career are over.

It is important to do as much research as possible into the venues that will support your music for your marketing plan. There is no point setting out a bunch of venues that will not hire you.

If you have toured, start with the venues that you have already done. Then add your desired venues that you hope to grow into as a result of the implementation of this marketing plan.

FACTOR puts a lot of emphasis on touring, so spend some time on this part of the plan. Be specific with the venues that you plan on playing at.

Other goals can include supporting a band that is further ahead or who can showcase you to the right audience.

Live performance on TV and radio is also a great way to get exposure to your audience.

Internet Promotion

When creating the online part of your plan, consider the following:

Along with live touring, internet promotion is probably the most important area to focus your marketing energy.

Having a website that is kept current is essential. Even if you do not have any ground-breaking news, don't stop refreshing your site. Do a blog about the recording of your album or your touring exploits. Your website should be clean and easy to navigate. It should not have a lot of fancy flash and other design issues that make access difficult. Allow for visitors to cut and paste your tour dates, bios and other printed materials.

Make sure that your site has music, links to videos, a store for CDs and merch, photo gallery, a place for the press to come and get band highlights and hi-res B&W and Colour pics, links to iTunes and other download retailers, bio, discography, contact information, lists of awards, tour dates, and links to other band sites.

In addition to your own website, make sure that you work your own Facebook, Twitter and YouTube pages. LinkedIn can be very helpful in reaching out to the music industry. Tailor your messaging to the service that you are using.

Utilize tools like the iTunes share function to send out links to your music to your fans. This function can be accessed by clicking on the pull down menu beside your album in the iTunes store. Simply click share to Twitter or Facebook and it should automatically start your message for you.

Consider advertising on Facebook. This is a cost effective way to get the word out to your fans. Facebook advertising allows you target your audience as well, which is fantastic. This would be a far more useful marketing spend than purchasing print advertising. Print advertising is extremely expensive and is not very effective with its declining readership.

Radio

For a FACTOR application, be very careful about radio, especially commercial radio. Commercial radio is very tight, so stating that you will service to all Rock, CHR, AAA, AC, Hot AC or other radio as the case may be far too general. For example, if you have a relationship with a local station such as 102.7 The PEAK in Vancouver, BC, then start there. Use your local contacts to build your story. Draft a plan that uses phases of success i.e., BC then Western Canada then Canada then the World.

Don't forget about the myriad of other radio options, including CBC, College Radio, Co-op Radio, Internet radio, Satellite Radio, Digital and Cable radio.

If radio is not realistic, then you may want to consider moving this topic lower down and starting with your best options for success, such as touring.

Press, Publicity and Print Ads

Hiring a publicist can be expensive. Be very careful that you have a reason to hire a publicist in the first place. Without a "hook", the publicist is going to have a hard time getting any press for you.

In the plan, research the dailies, weeklies, magazines and other periodicals that feature artists of your genre. Think outside the box – if you can be featured in a lifestyle magazine that matches your audience demographic, then go for it. If you have a publicist, ask him or her to get features outside of the norm.

Reviews and interviews are free. Buying print ads are very expensive. The more press that you can get, the better. If you can, make sure that your website address is featured in any article. Then fans can find you.

A good publicist can help secure television and radio appearances such as Urban Rush in Vancouver or Global News. Also, many stations such as the Peak will allow artists to come and play unplugged sets on air. This is a great way to promote your act.

Music Videos

As mentioned, the days of MTV and Much Music being instrumental in an artist's career are gone. Spending tens of thousands of dollars on a music video in most cases is a waste of money.

That is not to say that visual content is not important. Far from it. Video content is essential to the marketing of any artist today. Most people are discovering new music online and especially on YouTube. You must have video content, but not necessarily the expensive videos of the past. Local artist Jeremy Fisher made a video for his single "Cigarette" for $50 on his iMac and the video has been viewed over 2.2 million times to date. Be creative and smart with your money.

Film & Television

Film and television placement can bring an artist huge exposure to a wider audience through the usage of their songs in hit television shows or films. Even minor hit TV shows or indie films can increase the public's awareness of an artist, which in turn can spur artist album sales and greater access to funding, touring opportunities, distribution, etc.

Music supervisors can be approached for placement in film and television shows. Look for them at various music conferences around the world. Get to know them…be nice! Events like the CMW/CMPA Synch Summit can be very helpful in order to meet influential music supervisors. There are songwriter showcases at TIFF and other film festivals. Music BC and other MIAs bring supervisors up from L.A., NY and Toronto. Take advantage of those opportunities.

If you are an indie artist who owns both the master and song copyrights, then you can offer one stop clearance to music supervisors. They really love that. There are directories out there, but the best thing you can do is really research what shows you might be suitable for and target those supervisors.

Retail & Distribution

Traditional retail sales have plummeted to the point that many retailers and distributors have gone into receivership. A&B Sound closed shop last year, Virgin Megastore left Vancouver, Tower Records went bankrupt, Fusion 3 and PHD distribution both went into receivership this year. The traditional retail market for CDs has collapsed. This must be taken into account in any marketing plan. How are you going to sell CDs? Most Cds are being sold off the stage now and not through retailers. Do you need a traditional distributor?

Online distribution, while not coming close to replacing traditional sales, has made some headway of late for monetizing digital sales. iTunes is the biggest online retailer and any digital releases must include iTunes. The easiest route to the myriad of online retailers is through aggregators such as The Orchard, CD Baby or TuneCore.

CHAPTER 4

RELEASE CHECKLIST

Prior to releasing any sound recordings to the public, consider the checklist set out below. In fact, many of the items on this checklist need to be taken care of months before the actual street release date, so if you can build these into your Business Plan timeline milestones, then you may find that you do not miss one of the key release requirements.

Distribution

How are you planning to get the release out? There are some easy ways to access online retailers like iTunes by using an aggregator such as Tunecore or CD Baby. Remember that just because you can select "world" for digital distribution, does not mean that you should. Make sure that you have a plan for whatever territory that you are releasing to. Also, consider that if you do get a label interested in another territory, they will want the digital rights. If you have released in their territory, the album would be considered "old" and you have to go through the hassle of trying to delete the album in that territory after the fact.

As far as physical distribution, with retailers going out of business around the world, you may not want to rush into a physical distribution deal. You really have to look at the advantage of doing so. Most of your CD sales will be off-the-stage and mail order.

Make sure that you give yourself sufficient time to set up the release, building in time to manufacture and ship product.

Band/Group/Ensemble Agreement

Band/Group/Ensemble agreement for live performance, songwriting, sales, merchandise, band name ownership, leaving members, new members;

Register sole proprietorship, partnership or limited company

Legal

Do you have a signed producer agreement?

Do you have a mechanical license for any cover songs recorded on your album (CMRRA for Canada)?

Do you have an agreement from any side-players on the recording clearly assigning their performance rights and agreeing that they did not write or co-write any of the songs (if applicable)?

Do you have a songwriting agreement that clearly addresses copyright ownership, administration and songwriting splits? This is particularly important if you co-write with songwriters outside of your band or group. If you can secure the right to administer the copyrights in the songs that would be ideal. Being able to sign film and TV synch licenses and deal with mechanical licensing could end up being a vital right to secure.

Composing/Songwriting

Determine composition/songwriter splits in writing (songwriting agreement); Register songs with SOCAN (work notification forms online SOCAN); Ensure that Private Copying royalties are being collected (i.e. sign agreement with SOCAN to collect these royalties);

Make sure that MAPL CANCON (see below) notifications are on all releases of the song for radio purposes;

Register musical work copyrights with Library of Congress in Washington, DC – this can be done concurrently with sound recording to save filing fees http://www.copyright.gov/register/ (and/or with Copyright Board of Canada which registers titles of songs http://www.cb-cda.gc.ca/info/registration-e.html);

Sound Recordings

Ensure that ISRC codes (from Connect Music Licensing formerly AVLA) are digitally encoded on the final master recording (keep these numbers for release information to online distributor);

Set up online release with plenty of time to allow for the tracks to get up online;

If the artist has a distributor, then find out what the distributor requires with part delivery.

Register tracks with Connect Music Licensing formerly AVLA (as label or sound recording owner) and ACTRA RACS or MROC (as performers, whether lead or sidemen) to ensure the artist receives both sides of the Neighbouring Rights revenue from radio play and the Private Copying Levy royalties;

Register tracks with Sound Exchange in order to receive royalties on digital cable and satellite radio play in the USA;

Register sound recordings with Library of Congress in Washington, DC - include songs as well to save on filing fees (sound recordings cannot be registered with Copyright Board of Canada);

Digital and CD artwork

For CDs, make sure that your graphic designer has design specs from manufacturer and that delivery is made precisely as required (otherwise your release manufacturing may be significantly delayed);

Place copyright notices on all formats released. If CD, then place © and (p) information on actual disk as well as tray card;

Ensure that there is sufficient contact information on all formats to reach the artist, management, label and/or publisher. This is important to ensure that in the event a third party wants to secure licensing, that the correct parties are approached;

MAPL CANCON notification on all physical formats and tray card. This is a graphic that tells radio whether you are considered Canadian Content. The breakdown is music (songwriter Canadian), artist (artist is Canadian), production (produced in Canada) and lyrics (lyricist is Canadian). You need to be able to black in at least 2 out of the four of these on the MAPL graphic to be considered CANCON. This is important because in most cases stations are required to play 35% Canadian music content;

Secure bar code (usually from manufacturer or distributor) and create catalogue number for all physical format releases; Bar code must appear on the tray card or back of the CD. Catalogue numbers are usually on the spine. If you do not have a CD spine, then this can be added to the tray card as well.

The tray card or back of the CD is important and should include (a) song titles and song times, (b) name of artist, (c) MAPL logo (blacked in where appropriate), (d) legal notices, (e) bar code, and (f) contact information.

Place producer and credit information on insert – credit should include producer, engineer, studio, mixer, songwriter credits, mastering house, photographer, graphic designer;

Use care with thank-yous to include individuals and companies who helped the artist; Place website address on all insert materials;

Make sure that all song titles with times are included on tray card – this is important, especially for radio and other third party uses that require the song times;

Secure any mechanical licenses prior to release (cover song licenses). If the artist is also the writer, then the artist can also provide this. If there are third party co-writes or covers are being released, then the artist/label can go to the CMRRA to secure the mechanical licenses:

<u>CMRRA Song Clearance</u> (note: if the co-writer is not published, then artists may have to secure a mechanical license directly from the co-writer by agreement). Manufacturers require mechanical licenses prior to pressing.

Marketing and Promotion

Create a marketing plan that sets out a clear strategy for marketing and promoting the artist, including radio, video, touring, online promotion, publicity and other such marketing initiatives;

Create a time-line for the release and marketing. Make sure that all components of the plan are implemented in a manner that maximizes the impact of the release;

Consider hiring a radio tracker to release and track radio for the artist; Consider hiring a publicist to help with the release and touring;

Create a website which has a place for fans to sign up for newsletters on the home page. Make sure that the content is current and kept current at all times. Keep away from heavy flash sites – allow for HTML cut and paste options. Create an area for hi-res photo downloads for press (pass protect if necessary). Make sure that there is an easy way to purchase product from the artist – Paypal or links to iTunes;

Create a presence online including Myspace, Facebook, Twitter, YouTube and all other services that may be effective to promote the artist. Be vigilant in responding to friends and fans. Always personalize and try to avoid mass emails or notices;

Consider monetizing your online marketing. For example, YouTube allows you to monetize by approving advertising on your YouTube videos. You will have to register with <u>Google AdSense</u>. Keep in mind, however that the expectation of revenue needs to be modest. It is estimated that you need approximately 1 million views to generate $1,500 of revenue from YouTube views.

Create a classy newsletter that gets sent out at least once per month via email; Work with agents to secure touring and support dates;

Apply for festivals and showcases through Sonic Bids or through an agent;

Make sure that all tracks are serviced to film, TV, and video game music supervisors for inclusion in productions.

Merchandise and off-the-stage sales

Consider the registration of the artist name and/or trade names or marks with Trade Mark Office. This is an online application that can be completed relatively cheaply. Note that over time, fees will increase for a registration and the process can take up to two years;

Put a lot of thought into the merchandise being offered. Stay simple and have only a few options to start. Once key successful merchandise has been established, then diversify into other merchandising choices. Do not over-extend inventory. Do not give away product unnecessarily as merchandise is more expensive than CDs.

It is very, very important to be able to prove your sales. FACTOR requires proof of sales for many of its programs. The most reliable is SoundScan. The cost is $500 per year and you need to file SoundScan sheets with SoundScan to have those sales registered. You will need to register your release with SoundScan SoundScan title regitration If you cannot get your sales registered with SoundScan then consider setting up another form of proof of sales. An inventory sheet signed by the venue owner or promoter of each show would be helpful, but may not work with FACTOR and other funders such as Radio Starmaker.

CHAPTER 5

BAND AGREEMENT

One of the biggest favours that you can do for yourself if you have a band is to have a band agreement. This is a written document that sets out your relative rights, responsibilities and duties to the band. It is a document that can govern the business relationship between you. The band agreement can help to balance the inequities amongst the band and to clearly articulate where everyone stands. The agreement can also allow the band to easily manage the copyrights that you will create as you work together. Below is a list of questions that I always give to artists prior to their first meeting with me as a lawyer to draft a band agreement. It is important to have a lawyer draft this agreement. If you do it yourselves, you may forget key considerations or draft wording in a way that may be interpreted by a judge in a different way than you may have intended.

LIST OF QUESTIONS

What is the purpose of the band? Recording, songwriting, touring, merchandising – one or all of the above?

Is this going to be a company (limited) or a partnership? Is the company or partnership registered? Keep in mind that if you do nothing that your band will probably be considered a partnership under Canadian laws (which vary from province to province). The rule of thumb is that a partnership makes sense until the band is profitable, then it makes sense to roll everything into a limited company for tax purposes.

What are the full names and addresses of each of the band members? This is important in order to ensure that you can give notice to members if an issue comes up.

Contributions? Money? Loans or investments? Payback? This is a big one, as often band members will put in different amounts of money depending on their means. If this is the case, you need to think about how you are going to deal with an unequal investment amongst the band.

Third party contributions? Loans or investment? Getting a family member or big fan to invest in the band is very common. You have to create a way to be fair in paying back people who lend the band money or invest. The difference between a loan and investment is that with a loan, you are normally obliged to pay it back with interest. With an investment, there is usually only an obligation to pay back from certain revenues, but the investor will get some kind of ongoing share of profit once the band is in this position. Lenders do not share in profit, but they get the security of repayment.

Group name. Who owns the band name? If someone leaves, what happens with the band name? This is a huge issue. Control of the band name is paramount. If someone leaves, the band name needs to stay with the remaining members. If this is not dealt with, then the leaving member could hold the band name up for months or years.

Copyrights? Are the masters and songs going to be owned by the company? One way to build in a little pressure valve is to have the publishing go to the band. That way the songwriters can stay as songwriters and the performers can share in some of the revenue. As far as the masters are concerned, it is good to figure out who owns the masters and how revenues are going to be split between the band.

Insurance? An obligation to maintain gear and liability insurance. Often, bands will ensure all of the band gear on the road, even if individual band members have their own gear. There are no set rules here. The most important thing is that the equipment is insured and the band has adequate third party liability coverage (for example, if a fan gets hurt at a gig).

Equipment? Owned by band or individuals? Leased to band? Repairs? Strings and sticks? Share in profits? Equal or unequal?

Limitations? No moonlighting, non-competition, agreeing to majority decisions?

Songwriting? What is the songwriting split? Is the band going to own the songs or the songwriters? This can be one of the most contentious issues in any band. Figure out a way to keep this fair. My advice is to split the songwriter credits as they actually are and allocate some revenue splitting through the publishing incomes. In this way, the songwriters stay as songwriters, but the band gets a taste of the revenues.

Group issues:

Leaving members, new members, temporary substitution of members, buying out members, death of members, disability of members, mental incapacity of members, family law orders, drug use or other addiction issues. This may seem a bit macabre, but members do leave and unfortunately, members can also pass away. It has happened to bands that I have worked with. It is sad, but without clear guidelines as to what happens if someone leaves for any reason, then it can affect the entire group.

Dissolving the band? What would cause the band to break up? Liabilities? Third parties or contracts?

APPENDICES

LINKS

INTRODUCTION

All of the hyperlinks set out below are available as a companion to this book at: http://www.adagiomusic.ca/a-career-in-music/.

Music BC: http://www.musicbc.org
Peak Performance project: http://www.peakperformanceproject.com/
FACTOR: http://www.factor.ca/
CIMA: http://www.cimamusic.ca/
CCMIA: http://ccmia.ca/
BreakOut West: http://breakoutwest.ca/

PART 1

CHAPTER 1

Youtube: http://www.youtube.com/
Twitter: https://twitter.com/
Facebook: http://facebook.com
Bandcamp: http://bandcamp.com/
Instagram: http://instagram.com

Hide the Wife, Hide the Kids: http://www.youtube.com/watch?v=hMtZfW2z9dw&feature=youtu.be

Friday: http://www.youtube.com/watch?v=kfVsfOSbJY0&feature=youtu.be

Marc LaFrance: http://www.delinquentrecords.com/

CHAPTER 2

Outliers: http://www.gladwell.com/
SOCAN: http://www.socan.ca/
SAC: http://www.songwriters.ca/
CCMIA: http://www.ccmia.ca/

Wide Mouth Mason: http://www.widemouthmason.com/

Songwriting Books:

http://murphyslawsofsongwriting.com/ http://www.amazon.com/How-Write-Hit-Song-5th/dp/1423441982/

http://www.amazon.com/Writing-Better-Lyrics-Pat-Pattison/dp/1582975779

http://www.amazon.com/exec/obidos/ASIN/063400638X

http://www.amazon.com/exec/obidos/ASIN/1582970858/

http://www.amazon.com/exec/obidos/ASIN/0306812657

http://www.amazon.com/exec/obidos/ASIN/0898791499 http://www.amazon.com/exec/obidos/ASIN/0823084221 http://www.amazon.com/exec/obidos/ASIN/0898795192/

CHAPTER 3

Mother Mother: http://mothermothersite.com/

CHAPTER 4

Metalwood: https://myspace.com/metalwoodjazz

Anna Netrebko: http://www.annanetrebko.com/

Said the Whale video: http://www.youtube.com/watch?v=SCRGlfKZNGw&feature=youtu.be

Dominique Fricot video: http://www.youtube.com/watch?v=a3bVwmOnLbk&feature=youtu.be

CHAPTER 5

Tom Jackson: http://tomjacksonproductions.com/

CHAPTER 6

High Tech, High Touch: http://www.naisbitt.com/
Music BC: http://www.musicbc.org/
Tourhub: http://tourhub.ca/
CCMIA: http://ccmia.ca/

COCA: http://www.coca.org/en/

SXSW: http://www.sxsw.com/

CMJ: http://www.cmj.com/
REEPERBAUHN: http://www.reeperbahnfestival.com/
FOLK ALLIANCE: http://www.folkalliance.org/
CMW: http://cmw.net/
BIG SOUND: http://www.qmusic.com.au/bigsound
BREAKOUT WEST: http://breakoutwest.ca/
ECMA: http://www.ecma.com/
M FOR MONTREAL: http://www.mformontreal.com/
THE GREAT ESCAPE: http://mamacolive.com/thegreatescape/
BREAKOUT WEST/WCMA: http://breakoutwest.ca/
PACIFIC CONTACT: http://bctouring.org/pacific-contact
CONTACT EAST: http://www.contacteast.ca/
CMJ: http://www.cmj.com/

THE FELDMAN AGENCY: http://www.feldman-agency.com/
THE AGENCY GROUP: http://www.theagencygroup.com
PAQUIN ENTERTAINMENT: http://www.paquinentertainment.com/

CHAPTER 7

SPOTIFY: https://www.spotify.com/
PANDORA: http://www.pandora.com
RDIO: http://www.rdio.com/

YOUTUBE: http://www.youtube.com/
MAILCHIMP: http://mailchimp.com/

TWITTER: https://twitter.com/
FACEBOOK: www.facebook.com
INSTAGRAM: http://instagram.com
SOUNDCLOUD: https://soundcloud.com/
BANDCAMP: http://bandcamp.com/
TUMBLR: http://www.tumblr.com

MOTHER MOTHER BLOG: http://mothermothersite.com/blog
THE LEFSETZ LETTER: http://www.lefsetz.com/

PAYPAL: https://www.paypal.com

BRIAN THOMPSON: http://www.thornybleeder.com/

GOLDEN EAGLE SNATCHES KID: http://www.youtube.com/watch?v=CE0Q904gtMI&feature=youtu.be

CIGARETTE VIDEO: http://www.youtube.com/watch?v=xGn0q1zoibw&feature=youtu.be

GOOGLE ADSENSE: http://www.google.com/adsense/start/#utm_source=ww-en-et-storefront_adsense&utm_campaign=en&utm_medium=et&subid=ww-en-et-storefront_adsense

GANGNAM STYLE: http://www.youtube.com/watch?v=9bZkp7q19f0

CLICKTOTWEET: clicktotweet.com/

HOOTSUITE: https://hootsuite.com/

MAILCHIMP: http://mailchimp.com/

DROPBOX: https://www.dropbox.com/
BOX: https://www.box.com/
HIGHTAIL:https://www.hightail.com

DAMN YOU AUTOCORRECT: http://www.damnyouautocorrect.com/

ERIK QUALMAN: http://www.socialnomics.net/

CHAPTER 8

GRANT LAWRENCE: http://grantlawrence.ca/

MALING FRIENDS WITH THE MEDIA: http://www.grantlawrence.com/speaking

SIGUR ROS VIDEO: http://www.youtube.com/watch?v=OIMGPlH4XPo&feature=youtu.be

DMDS: http://v5.dmds.com/DMDS.WebApp.Public/DefaultFrame.aspx

RDR MUSIC GROUP: http://www.rdrmusic.ca/

BDS REGISTRATION:http://www.bdsradio.ca/

TANDEM TRACKS: https://www.facebook.com/tandemtracks
FRONTSIDE: http://www.frontsidegroup.com/

CBC 1: http://www.cbc.ca/programguide/daily/today/cbc_radio_one
CBC 2: http://music.cbc.ca/#/radio2/
CBC 3: http://music.cbc.ca/#/radio3/

PUBLICISTS:

http://killbeatmusic.com/
http://fritzmedia.ca/
http://strutentertainment.com/
http://www.hypemusiconline.com/
http://www.modmaypromotions.com/

CHAPTER 9

CCMIA: http://www.ccmia.ca/
CIMA: http://www.cimamusic.ca/

MUSIC ONTARIO: http://www.cimamusic.ca/

TOURHUB: http://tourhub.ca/

BREAKOUT WEST AND WCMAS: http://breakoutwest.ca/

FACTOR: http://www.factor.ca/
RADIO STARMAKER: https://www.starmaker.ca/
CCMIA: http://www.ccmia.ca/
CANADA COUNCIL: http://www.canadacouncil.ca/
PEAK PERFORMANCE PROJECT: http://www.peakperformanceproject.com

PPP BANDS:

http://www.wearethecity.ca/
http://saidthewhale.com/ http://kyprios.com/
http://currentswell.com/
http://theboombooms.com/
http://www.thematineemusic.com/
http://www.jordanklassen.com/
http://dominiquefricot.com/
http://bendsinisterband.com/
http://dearrouge.com/

INDIEGOGO: http://www.indiegogo.com/
KICKSTARTER: http://www.kickstarter.com/
PLEDGEMUSIC http://www.pledgemusic.com

CHAPTER 10

HILARY GRIST: http://www.kickstarter.com/
GIL BRUVEL: http://www.bruvel.com/
MYTHOS: http://www.mythosmusic.com

CHAPTER 11

SOCAN: http://www.socan.ca/
CMRRA: http://www.cmrra.ca/
HARRY FOX AGENCY: http://www.harryfox.com/

LIBRARY OF CONGRESS USA: http://www.copyright.gov/eco/
CANADIAN COPYRIGHT REGISTRATION: www.cb-cda.gc.ca/

CONNECT MUSIC LICENSING (formerly AVLA): http://www.connectmusiclicensing.ca/

MAPL: http://www.crtc.gc.ca/eng/info_sht/r1.htm
SOCAN: http://www.socan.ca/

RACS/ACTRA: http://www.actra.ca/racs/

MROC: http://musiciansrights.ca/
SOCAN: http://www.socan.ca/
CMRRA: http://www.cmrra.ca/
HARRY FOX AGENCY: http://www.harryfox.com/

SOUNDSCAN REGISTRATION: http://titlereg.soundscan.com/soundscantitlereg/

SPOTIFY: https://www.spotify.com

DROPBOX: https://www.dropbox.com/
BOX: https://www.box.com/

RE:SOUND: http://www.resound.ca/

US Tax EIN: http://www.irs.gov/Businesses/Small-Businesses-&-Self-Employed/Apply-for-an- Employer-Identification-Number-(EIN)-Online

US Treaty declaration for royalties - W8BEN: http://www.irs.gov/pub/irs-pdf/fw8ben.pdf
SOUND EXCHANGE: http://www.soundexchange.com/
CONNECT MUSIC LICENSING (formerly AVLA): http://www.connectmusiclicensing.ca/
ARTS AND CRAFTS: http://www.arts-crafts.ca/

CHAPTER 12

HUEY LEWIS: http://hueylewisandthenews.com/
DAN MANGAN: http://www.danmanganmusic.com/

PART 2

CHAPTER 1 COPYRIGHT ACT

COPYRIGHT ACT (CANADA) http://www.parl.gc.ca/HousePublications/Publication.aspx? Language=E&Mode=1&DocId=5697419

WIPO: http://www.wipo.int/copyright/en/treaties.htm

USA DIGITAL COPYRIGHT: http://www.copyright.gov/legislation/dmca.pdf

CHAPTER 3 MARKETING PLANS

High Tech, High Touch: http://www.naisbitt.com/
FACTOR: http://www.factor.ca/
102.7 THE PEAK: http://www.thepeak.fm/

CDBABY: http://www.cdbaby.com/
TUNECORE: http://www.tunecore.com/
THE ORCHARD: http://www.theorchard.com/

CHAPTER 4 RELEASE CHECKLIST

TUNECORE: http://www.tunecore.com/
CDBABY: http://www.cdbaby.com/

SOCAN: http://www.socan.ca/
LIBRARY OF CONGRESS: http://www.copyright.gov/
CANADIAN COPYRIGHT OFFICE: http://www.cb-cda.gc.ca/
Connect Music Licensing: http://www.avla.ca/
Connect Music Licensing: http://www.avla.ca/
ACTRA RACS: http://www.actra.ca/racs/
MROC: http://musiciansrights.ca/
SOUND EXCHANGE: http://www.soundexchange.com/

CMRRA: http://www.cmrra.ca/Mechanical_Licensing/mechanical_licensing.html

GOOGLE ADSENSE: http://www.google.com/adsense/start/#utm_source=ww-en-et-storefront_adsense&utm_campaign=en&utm_medium=et&subid=ww-en-et-storefront_adsense

SOUNDSCAN VENUE SALES:
http://nielsen.com/content/dam/nielsen/en_ca/documents/pdf/fact_sheets/Venue%20Sales%20Canada.pdf

SOUNDSCAN REGISTRATION: http://titlereg.soundscan.com/soundscantitlereg/

CONTACT AND BOOKING

Bob D'Eith is available to present seminars, lectures or panels based on the contents of this book. For booking information, please contact info@adagiomusic.ca.

More information on Bob as a an author and about his various roles in the music industry can be found at:

www.bobdeith.com

with links to:

Law: www.bcmusiclaw.com,
Label, Publishing and Consulting: www.adagiomusic.ca.
Artist: www.mythosmusic.com,
Music Association: www.musicbc.org
Blog: http://www.tumblr.com/blog/acareerinmusic
Microblog: https://twitter.com/bobdeith
Ongoing news:https://www.facebook.com/bob.deith

Bob D'Eith professional background

Bob D'Eith has been involved in the music industry for twenty-four years in various capacities: entertainment lawyer (D'Eith & Company), two time JUNO Award nominated recording artist (Rymes with Orange and Mythos), studio owner, label and publisher (Adagio Media).

For the past eleven years, Bob has been the executive director of the Music BC Industry Association (Music BC), a non-profit society dedicated to the development of music and the music industry in BC. Music BC administers the award winning Peak Performance Project and is also the FACTOR affiliated office for BC.

He is on the board of the CIMA (Canadian Independent Music Association) (past-executive). Bob is also on FACTOR's National Advisory Board (past chair). Bob was the executive chair of the Host Committee for the Vancouver 2009 JUNO Awards. Bob is a director of the Canadian Council of Music Industry Associations (CCMIA).

38382926R00062

Made in the USA
Charleston, SC
08 February 2015